Face to Face

Second Edition

Face to Face

Communication, Culture, and Collaboration

Second Edition

Virginia Vogel Zanger

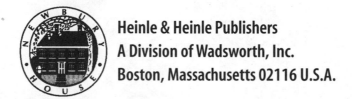

Heinle & Heinle Publishers
A Division of Wadsworth, Inc.
Boston, Massachusetts 02116 U.S.A.

Heinle & Heinle Publishers is a division of Wadsworth, Inc.

Manufactured in the United States of America

Publisher: Stanley J. Galek
Editor: Erik Gundersen
Associate Editor: Lynne Telson Barsky
Editorial Production Manager: Elizabeth Holthaus
Production Editor: Kristin M. Thalheimer
Photo Coordinator: Martha Leibs-Heckly
Manufacturing Coordinator: Jerry Christopher
Photographers: Carol Palmer and Andrew Brilliant
Illustrator: Devera Ehrenberg
Interior Designer and Compositor: Greta D. Sibley
Cover Designer: Bortman Design Group/Howie Green
Cover Artist: Craig Smallish

ISBN: 0-8384-39543

10   9   8

To my husband, Mark, who has supported

this project in every possible way.

Acknowledgments

This book would not have been possible without the contributions of a great many people. The first edition was developed with the encouragement and counsel of Pixie Martin, Consuelo Inchaustegui, Ned Seelye, Ralph Radell, Jaime Wurzel, Robert Kohls, Van Lan Truong, Maria Perez, Libby Shufro, Richard Berger, Jose Masso, Ellen Glanz, Miguel Satut, and Carmen Judith Nine Curt. The second edition has benefited immeasurably from the suggestions of Cathy Wong, Charles Skidmore, Thuy-Phuong Nguyen, Raynel Shepard, Ping Ann, Joan Hamilton, Junko Takasawa, Kazuko Tonoike, Sheila Becker, Noboru Sawahashi, and Shinichi Nakamura. I would also like to thank the many ESL teachers who used the first edition of *Face to Face* in their classrooms — including my mother, Helen Vogel — for their recommendations and support. Among these, Jonathan Seely, Kevin Keating, C. A. Edington, James Rupp, and Ruth Gray reviewed the second edition at various stages and made many excellent suggestions. I am most grateful to Steve Molinsky, whose encouraging words came at critical stages of both the first and second editions of *Face to Face*. I hope that the book does, in fact, make a contribution to the field that he envisioned. This edition of *Face to Face* owes a great deal to David and Roger Johnson, Marian Leibowitz, Judy Winn-Bell Olsen, Robert Slavin, and Spencer Kagan, cooperative learning trainers whose ideas I've adapted here to the needs of the ESL classroom. I would also like to thank my students over the years for both their practical suggestions and continuing inspiration.

Both editions of this book have been blessed along the way by editors with heart: Jim Brown, Elizabeth Lentz, Kathy Ossip, Lynne Telson Barsky, and, most especially, Erik Gundersen. This edition would not be the same without the enthusiasm and artistry of photographers Carol Palmer and Andy Brilliant.

Table of Contents

PREFACE: TO THE TEACHER...1

STARTING OFF: AN INTRODUCTION 12

Chapter 1 ....BODY LANGUAGE 18

Chapter 2 ....SCHOOL..40

Chapter 3 ....PROVERBS 58

Chapter 4 ....MANNERS..78

Chapter 5 ....WORK 98

Chapter 6 ....FAMILY..116

Chapter 7 ....MALES & FEMALES 136

Chapter 8 ....TIME..162

Chapter 9 ....MONEY...180

Chapter 10 .....EATING 200

PHOTOGRAPHY CREDITS 222

To the Teacher

Have you ever asked your ESL students to keep a 24-hour log, noting how often and with whom they speak English? You may be surprised — as I was — to find out just how limited the daily interactions with native English-speakers are for many. Such isolation may be the biggest barrier that many students face in their struggle to become fluent in English. The first edition of *Face to Face* has given intermediate and advanced level ESL students an opportunity to break through this barrier in a systematic way. The new edition has been almost completely rewritten to help you become even more effective in improving the quality and quantity of your students' interactions in English.

OVERVIEW

The central idea of the book is simple: to learn about North American culture, firsthand, from native speakers of English. A Vietnamese student who used the first edition of *Face to Face* summarized the impact of using this approach: "We know American culture more, so when we go out and talk to Americans, we're not confused." In the process of cross-cultural exploration, students working with *Face to Face* develop their English by using the language in a relevant and meaningful context.

For most of this century, cultural anthropologists have sought to learn about other cultures *from an insider's perspective* by means of the ethnographic interview. *Face to Face* has adapted this technique to allow ESL students to gain an insider's perspective on American culture. In each chapter, students explore one cultural topic, such as work, family, or school. They learn about the cross-cultural dimensions of the issue by interviewing each other and a North American informant. A variety of other activities, such as case studies, analysis of interview data in pairs and in small groups, and journal writing stimulate further exploration of the chapter topics and ensure that students get the most out of their interviews. *Face to Face* has been used by intermediate and advanced ESL students in university, adult education, and high school classes around the world.

....
GOALS

Face to Face is about communication, culture, and collaboration. These are the goals of the book, and they function interactively. Each chapter takes advantage of students' interest in practical, everyday cultural issues, such as North American dating customs, to stimulate meaningful communication with classmates and native speakers of English. Collaborating with classmates in pairs and in small groups, students develop fluency by using their second language in a meaningful way, while also gaining new cultural insights.

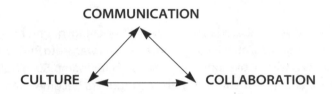

1. Communication. Reflecting on the ways in which *Face to Face* had improved her fluency in English, one student wrote: "I *had* to practice my English — the book *made* us talk to Americans." The text develops communicative competence by structuring conversations in English on a regular basis with native English-speakers and fellow classmates within a controlled format and in a supportive atmosphere. Exercises prepare students linguistically and culturally for each interview. The interview itself is structured carefully: students ask cultural informants specific questions about both customs and values. The questions themselves are thought-provoking but non-threatening. Some are open-ended and in every interview students have to formulate one question (or more) on their own.

Face to Face was developed as a way to get students to practice oral English in a meaningful context, to help them to develop fluency in authentic, rather than "classroom" English. Students have used this book to help each other solve the mysteries of culture while coming to terms with their own culture shock. The new edition gives students the opportunity to work on basic communication skills within the context of exploring cultural themes. Students engage in process writing activities such as outlining, cognitive mapping, journal writing, and peer editing within the cultural topics of each chapter. Other activities target the development of critical thinking. For example, graphing, charting, and analyzing interview data help students to differentiate between fact and opinion, avoid overgeneralizations, draw accurate conclusions, and compare and contrast. Students develop their public speaking skills through debates, reporting from small group discussions, and oral reports. The book introduces students to idiomatic and colloquial expressions related to each cultural unit in order to enhance their ability to communicate with native speakers around the interview topic.

Increasing both quantity and quality of contact with native English speakers through *Face to Face* interviews seems to increase students' confidence in their own abilities to communicate in English (Zanger, 1987). One student interviewed a number of Americans using the first edition and commented, "Now I really enjoy and feel comfortable speaking more than I used to because I am not afraid to speak English now. At the beginning of the school year I was really scared to speak English. In my mind at that time I was afraid that if I spoke English, nobody would understand me."

2. Culture.

Anthropologists estimate that language accounts for only 35 percent of communication (Birdwhistell, 1970). *Face to Face* introduces students to some of the cultural factors that can affect the remaining 65 percent: non-verbal communication, basic cultural assumptions, and values. These vital aspects of what anthropologists call "deep culture" can mean the difference between *knowing* a language and *knowing how to use one,* the difference between understanding *what is talked about* versus *what is said,* and, ultimately, the difference between *understanding* and *misunderstanding* (Hickey, 1980).

Intercultural proficiency involves more than an understanding of another culture. More important, perhaps, is an awareness of one's own cultural conditioning. As anthropologist Ruth Benedict writes: "We do not see the lens through which we look." For this reason, many of the exercises in *Face to Face* are designed to help each student explore his or her own cultural background, and thus become more aware of the ways in which perceptions and communication patterns are influenced by culture.

Face to Face also helps students become more culturally proficient by encouraging them to see the diversity within American culture and within their own cultures. On any given topic, the opinions of a range of Americans — as many as the class can interview — are surveyed. A diversity of opinions and customs are bound to emerge, and students are asked to analyze these in several ways. They identify the most typical responses as well as the atypical ones, and discuss how these reflect the dominant American culture. Students are encouraged to look at the heterogeneity of American culture. They become conscious of factors such as social class, age, region, ethnicity, religion, race, and gender and how these elements can affect variation from the dominant American culture.

The new edition of *Face to Face* has added exercises that address aspects of "practical culture" to help students negotiate daily life in the United States. Social customs such as table manners, terms of endearment, roommate searches, and when to say "excuse me" are introduced and practiced through the book's case studies and interactive activities. Furthermore, the *Interview Tips* in each chapter provide students with concrete advice about how to avoid specific misunderstandings which can impede cross-cultural communication.

3. Collaboration.

Hundreds of studies of classes using the cooperative learning indicate that this method fosters language development, increases academic achievement, breaks down racial and ethnic barriers, and increases students' enjoyment of the subject matter (Slavin, 1990). ESL teachers will not be surprised at research findings which suggest that language minority students in particular seem to benefit from working in small groups (Kagan, 1986).

In fact, this is certainly the reason why ESL teachers have been pairing students up and having them work in small groups for years. Despite the rewards, however, there are many potential pitfalls. Some students may dominate discussions, for example, while others remain silent. Some students may feel left-out, or may insist on working only with friends. Inevitably, some students prefer to work by themselves. Worse, even small groups can degenerate into noisy chaos, leaving the teacher frustrated and powerless. Some students may even feel that the teacher has abandoned them.

The cooperative learning movement has researched "pairwork" or "groupwork" in order to develop solutions to some of these problems. In *Face to Face,* I have adapted some of these classroom management techniques and woven them into the text to help you avoid some of the common pitfalls. Among the highlights:

- To encourage students to work together, many exercises instruct students to produce a single product, such as a joint worksheet, list, report, or even drawing. Ask each student to sign these joint efforts to show individual participation.
- To make sure that all students bring something to the group, every collaborative activity begins with a directive for students to think or write about a series of questions on their own. This individual reflective work lays a foundation for subsequent activities in pairs or small groups.
- To encourage all students to participate once they join a small group, the book directs each individual to take on a role, such as group secretary, reporter, group leader, timekeeper, and even praiser. The book assigns students to these roles according to different criteria and tasks are rotated frequently. Similarly, many pairwork activities direct partners to take turns doing the writing or interviewing so that each person gets an equal chance.
- To make ESL classes more fun for both students and teachers, the pairwork and groupwork activities are varied in each chapter. Some call for pairs to quiz each other; others direct students to express their positions on a given question by standing on opposite sides of the classroom; while others direct students to rotate partners during language drills in two concentric circles facing each other.
- To help students improve their group process, some exercises and journal assignments ask them to evaluate how their small group functions and how they function within it. Cooperative learning researchers have found that explicit attention to improving group process is essential for developing and maintaining small group productivity. Additional suggestions are made at the end of the next section.

Virginia Vogel Zanger

ORGANIZATION OF THE TEXT

Starting Off is a short but crucial introduction to *Face to Face.* It explains the rationale of the book in simple language, introduces the concept of culture, and asks students to identify their own questions about American culture. Compile these questions into a class list (without identifying names), discuss them, and save them to review together at the end of the semester. These questions will help motivate the class once students realize that the book is a useful tool to help them find answers to their own questions.

Starting Off is important because it introduces an anthropological definition of culture that is used throughout the book, and raises the concept of deep culture. It also sets some basic ground rules for studying other cultures: the dangers of overgeneralization and ethnocentrism. It is quite useful if students understand these concepts well and can recognize them clearly as they are bound to occur in subsequent activities.

The ten chapters in *Face to Face* focus on topics that are reflected in the chapter titles, e.g. Body Language and Time. All chapters share a similar general format, consisting of the following sections:

- Warm-Up
- Preparation
- Interviews and Analysis
- Additional Activities

Activities within this format vary from chapter to chapter. The heart of each chapter is the Interviews and Analysis section. If you do not have time to complete all activities in a given chapter, think about just covering the exercises in this section.

1. Warm-Up. The cultural topic of each chapter is introduced by a photograph followed by questions which direct students to reflect individually and jot down some notes *(Think About This)*. Students are then asked to share their reflections with a partner and together arrive at some synthesis by graphing, charting, drawing, or listing their reponses to other questions. Some of these pairwork activities culminate in a sharing activity with the entire class; others direct pairs to share with another pair. The purpose of these chapter openers is to engage students in an initial discussion about some aspect of the general topic to be explored. Throughout each chapter, additional photos and graphics, followed by questions and pairwork activities, provide further opportunities for discussion about the chapter topic.

2. Preparation for the two interviews to be done in each chapter includes the following activities:

- **Journal.** The journal writing assignments at the beginning and end of each chapter encourage students to reflect on the chapter topic and relate it to their own lives. You may respond to students' entries in writing or choose to keep journal entries private. As always, the purpose of journal writing here is to develop students' ideas as freely as possible without fear of correction. It might be wise to explain the special function of journal writing to students so that they do not feel ignored or cheated when journals are returned without the grammatical corrections which they may expect. In a conversation class, you may want to try a variation on standard journal writing, the audio-journal, where students tape record their reflections on journal topics. A second journal assignment is included in each chapter, just before Additional Activities are listed.
- **Case Study.** These are short critical incidents which introduce the chapter topic in a cross-cultural context. They feature dialogue with colloquial expressions related to the chapter's cultural topic, in order to prepare students for vocabulary which they may encounter in later interviews with North American informants. The case study in each

chapter is followed by a GLOSSARY, QUESTIONS for individual work, and PAIRWORK exercises. The case study may be assigned for homework or read in class. Questions check comprehension and often ask students to relate the themes to their own cross-cultural experiences. Pairwork activities direct students to work with the glossed vocabulary and analyze the reading.

- **Background Reading with Glossary and Questions.** These essays provide explanations and interpretations of case studies and introduce key issues related to the chapter topic. The book encourages students to answer the comprehension questions in pairs, but can also be assigned as homework.

3. Interviews and Analysis is the section which includes, in most chapters:

- **Interview Tip and Exercise.** These tips, one per chapter, train students to get the most out of their interviews by focusing on specific skills, such as note-taking, maintaining eye contact, and setting time limits. In some chapters, the interview tips introduce supplementary vocabulary which relates to the interview topic. To reinforce the skills and vocabulary, pairwork exercises follow each tip.
- **In-class Questionnaire.** The first questionnaire in each chapter is a list of questions about the chapter topic to structure students' interviews with each other. The *In-class Questionnaire* is almost identical to the *Out-of-class Questionnaire* which the students will use to interview a North American. The purpose of the *In-class Questionnaire* is three-fold: 1) to give students practice asking the questions which they will be asking an American later on; 2) to give them an opportunity to learn about a classmate's culture; and 3) to deepen their awareness of their own cultural backgrounds.
- **Out-of-class Questionnaire** is a list of questions similar to those on the *In-class Questionnaire,* and is intended to give structure to students' interviews with a North American informant. With the help of a partner, students are asked to add one question of their own to the questionnaire. There is space at the end of each *Out-of-class Questionnaire* for students to note down any new vocabulary words that come up during the interview. Remind students to have their informants sign their names in the space provided at the end of the questionnaire to show that they have completed the interview assignment. In some chapters, students are asked to write down some background information about their American informants. Students will use this data later to analyze their informants' responses.

The above format varies in several chapters. The first two chapters, for example, encourage students to work with their partner and interview a North American informant together. In chapters 5, 7 and 10, students are offered a choice of questionnaires to guide their interviews with North Americans. After choosing a topic of interest, students use the appropriate questionnaire and work together in teams to analyze their data. The last chapter in the book gives students practice in formulating half of the interview questions.

- **Analysis on Your Own, Analysis in Pairs, Analysis in a Small Group, and Analysis in Class.** These activities, varied in each chapter, guide students to reflect on, analyze, and draw conclusions about the cross-cultural data which they gather from their interviews with each other and with an American informant. They also provide students with additional support in interviewing, as students have opportunities to share their experiences with the interview process as well as the content.

  The class discussion, facilitated by the teacher and structured with guide questions, help students in several ways. First, it includes a teacher's perspective, which is essential for helping students understand American responses. This is an excellent time for you to help steer students away from inaccurate or biased conclusions. A further benefit of the full class discussion is that the comparison of answers with classmates allows everyone to view the diversity of American culture.

4. **Additional Activities** suggests further ways to approach the topic, such as:

- **Role-plays, Readings, Graphing, Writing Assignments, Additional Interviews, Library Research, Outlining, Idea-mapping, Debates, Field Trips, and other activities.** View these as optional activities to vary and spice up classwork and homework assignments. They expand on and supplement students' understanding of the chapter topic. They also afford students further development of reading, writing, listening, speaking, and critical thinking skills. Some introduce specific survival skills for living in the United States.

Questions and Answers about Using Face to Face

1. How much time should be allotted to using *Face to Face?*

This varies according to the nature and length of the class, whether or not the book is used as the main text, and how much homework is assigned. However, unless you are using *Face to Face* as the main text in a year-long course, you and your students will be frustrated if you attempt to get through all the activities in every chapter. Choose which chapters your class will work on according to your students' areas of interest. You will have a better sense of what these are after students complete the question-writing exercise in *Starting Off*. Within any given chapter, be flexible about choosing those exercises and activities which meet your course goals as well as the needs and interests of your students. For example, if you are using the book in a conversation course, you may want to skip many of the process writing activities. Or you may decide to assign students to study and practice the interviewing tip in a chapter which the class will not have time to cover (see below). It is a good idea to let students know that you are not planning to finish the entire book, so that they do not feel cheated. Encourage them to continue using the book after the course has ended.

Some teachers have used *Face to Face* for individualized student learning projects or assigned it to a small group of advanced students. Individual students do not have as much of an opportunity to learn about the diversity of North American culture as would an entire class using the book. It is, therefore, particularly important for you to monitor students' conclusions about North American culture, based on their individual interviews.

2. Does the order in which chapters are covered matter?

It is best to begin with Chapter 1, Body Language, because it introduces students to the process of interviewing an American informant by having them conduct a joint interview in pairs (as does Chapter 2). The first chapter is also a nice introduction to the study of culture because the topic is fun and less threatening. The last chapter, Eating, should be covered after students have covered other chapters, since it calls upon them to write many of the questions on the questionnaires. Select the rest of the chapters in any order you want.

3. How do students react to the assignment of interviewing an American?

They react differently, as they do to everything else. One student called it "an adventure." Another said she became "anxious," especially the first time. Based on the experiences of students using the first edition of *Face to Face,* the second edition has been rewritten to provide additional support for students who may feel timid about interviews. For example, each chaper introduces and provides practice on specific interviewing tips. Some highlights are:

- Chapter 1: Look Your Informant in the Eye
- Chapter 2: Follow-Up Questions
- Chapter 3: Taking Notes During an Interview
- Chapter 4: Helping Your Informant to Relax with Warm-Up Questions
- Chapter 8: Timing Your Interview
- Chapter 10: Making Up Good Interview Questions

You may wish to work on some of these skills out of order.

Shy students will gain confidence after conducting their first interview of an American with a partner, as directed in Chapters 1 and 2. If some students are too apprehensive about completing subsequent interview assignments on their own, be flexible about permitting joint interviews. The second edition includes other forms of peer support to help students gain confidence in their interviews with North Americans: interviewing a partner, discussions with a partner about the interview plans, and evaluations of the interview process in pairs and in small groups.

Be prepared for some student resistance to completing the North American informant interview assignment. Remember that for many students, it is a completely unfamiliar type of assignment. Many students are not used to taking this kind of social initiative. One teacher recommended that it is important to be "authoritarian": make it clear to students that you expect everyone to complete the interview assignment. Be supportive, but firm. Students will be grateful if you give them the necessary push.

4. Who should students interview out of class?

This can be a sticky question. Because it is important to emphasize that North Americans include people from diverse backgrounds, it would be a mistake to allow students to interview only those born in the United States. On the other hand, if students try to interview only friends and relatives from their own background to dodge the intent of the assignment, you should insist on more diversity. Try setting a criterion of a minimum number of years spent in the United States.

To head off just such problems, you might want to take the initiative to bring North American volunteers in to class, especially for students' first interviews. If you do not have enough volunteers for one-on-one interviews, divide students into groups to conduct joint interviews. Recruit North American student volunteers by arranging for them to get some course credit. Another solution is to pair your class up with a North American class studying something related to one of the chapter themes. For example, a nutrition class could gain valuable cross-cultural information and perspectives by participating in mutual interviews about eating, in Chapter 10. If students are responsible for finding their own interview subjects, encourage them to seek potential volunteers where they live, work, and study. They need to ask volunteers to donate a half hour of their time to help with a homework assignment.

5. What about stereotyping and overgeneralizing?

Stereotyping and generalizing are normal cognitive processes which we all use. They become dysfunctional, however, when rigid stereotypes and overgeneralizations prevent us from paying attention to data that doesn't fit our preconceptions. Furthermore, *negative* stereotyping creates barriers that limit the amount of information we receive.

As a teacher using *Face to Face* with your class, an important part of your job is to help students avoid overgeneralizing and to recognize negative stereotypes. The book is set up to help you to do that. The *Starting Off* chapter will introduce your students to the concept of overgeneralizations. Various exercises in the chapters cover related topics, such as differentiating between fact and opinion. Most importantly, students are asked to compare the data from their interviews with the data collected by their classmates before drawing any conclusions about North American culture. Guided by questions in the text for whole group discussions, it is up to you to help your students become more aware of the breadth of diversity within North American culture, and to teach them to be cautious in making generalizations about it or any other culture. It falls upon your shoulders to help them to recognize their own ethnocentrism by reminding them that though cultures may differ, none is superior or inferior to any other.

6. Can the book be used in EFL classes?

Teachers have adapted the first edition for successful use with their classes abroad. Some teachers who are native English-speakers have had their classes interview them. In other situations, teachers have made special arrangements to bring in native English-speakers or other North Americans for their students to interview. This can work quite successfully in colleges that have programs for North Americans studying abroad.

····················
SUGGESTED READINGS

≡ On Culture

Some of the following texts discuss cross-cultural issues at levels of interest and language more appropriate for teachers, while others are geared to an international student audience.

— Althen, Gary. *American Ways: A Guide for Foreigners.* Yarmouth, ME: Intercultural Press, 1988.

— Claire, Elizabeth. *What's So Funny: A Foreign Student's Introduction to American Humor.* Rochelle Park, NJ: Eardley Publications, 1984.

— Gaston, Jan. *Cultural Awareness Teaching Techniques.* Brattleboro, VT: Pro Lingua Associates, 1984.

— Hall, Edward T. *The Hidden Dimension.* Garden City, NY: Doubleday, 1966.

— Lewis, Tom & Robert Jungman, eds. *On Being Foreign: Culture Shock in Short Fiction, An International Anthology.* Yarmouth, ME: Intercultural Press, 1986.

— Manton, Judy. *You and Your Child's School: For the ESL Parent.* Syracuse, NY: New Reader's Press, 1991.

— Mothershead, Alice Bonzi. *Dining Customs around the World.* Garett Park, MD: Garett Park Press, 1982.

— Morris, Desmond, Peter Collett, Peter Marsh, & Marie O'Shaughnessy. *Gestures.* Briarcliff Manor, NY: Stein and Day, 1980.

— Nine Curt, Carmen Judith. *Non-Verbal Communication.* Fall River, MA: National Assessment and Dissemination Center, 1976.

— Seelye, H. Ned. *Teaching Culture.* Lincolnwood, IL: National Textbook Company, 1984.

— Stewart, Edward C. & Milton J. Bennett. *American Cultural Patterns: A Cross-Cultural Perspective.* Yarmouth, ME: Intercultural Press, 1991.

— Wurzel, Jaime. *Toward Multicultural Awareness.* Yarmouthport, ME: Intercultural Press, 1985.

≡ On Cooperative Learning Methods

The following books are excellent guides that will help you carry out the collaborative activities in *Face to Face.*

— Brubacher, Mark, Ryder Payne & Kemp Rickett. *Perspectives on Small Group Learning: Theory and Practice.* Oakville, Ontario, Canada: Rubicon Publishing Co., 1990.

— *Cooperative Learning* (magazine). 136 Liberty Street, Santa Cruz, CA 95060.

— Johnson, David, et. al. *Circles of Learning.* New Brighton, MI: Interaction Book Co., 1984.

— Kagan, Spencer. *Cooperative Learning Resources for Teachers.* San Juan Capistrano, CA: Resources for Teachers, 1990.

····················
SUGGESTED VIDEOS

Students' understanding of cultural topics covered in *Face to Face* will be greatly enhanced by the showing and discussion of selected commercial videos in class. For example, consider showing the satirical Japanese film *Tampopo* in conjunction with the chapter on eating, or *Parenthood* when the class is investigating topics of family life. The following videos, which are not available in video stores, complement topics in the text:

— *Breaking Through: Portraits of Winners.* Five adults from Spanish-speaking backgrounds discuss the development of their careers in the United States. 30 minutes. Available for rental or purchase from: The Network, Andover, MA.

— *Cold Water.* International college students reflect on culture shock and experts on cross-cultural adaptation elaborate. 48 minutes. Available for rental or purchase from: Intercultural Press, Yarmouth, ME.

— *How We Feel: Hispanic Students Speak Out.* High school students from a variety of Spanish-speaking backgrounds discuss their experiences of schooling in the United States. 15 minutes. Available for purchase from: Landmark Films, Falls Church, VA, 1990.

— *Working in the U. S. A.* An introduction to the culture of the American workplace. 30 minutes. Available for rental or purchase from: Copeland Griggs Productions, San Francisco, CA.

PUBLICATIONS CITED

1. Birdwhistell, Ray L. *Kinesics and Context.* Philadelphia, PA: University of Pennsylvania Press, 1970.
2. Cummins, Jim. *Empowering Minority Students.* Sacramento, CA: California Association for Bilingual Education, 1989.
3. Hall, Edward. *The Silent Language.* Garden City, NY: Anchor Books, 1973.
4. Hickey, Leo. "Ethnography for Language Learners." In *Foreign Language Annals,* no. 6, 1980.
5. Kagan, Spencer. "Cooperative Learning and Sociocultural Factors in Schooling." In *Beyond Language: Social and Cultural Factors in Schooling Language Minority Students.* Los Angeles, CA: Evaluation, Dissemination and Assessment Center, California State University, 1986.
6. Schumann, John. "Social and Psychological Factors in Second Language Acquisition." Ed. J. Richards. *Understanding Second and Foreign Language Learning.* Rowley, MA: Newbury House Publishers, Inc., 1978. (ed.), *Second Language Acquisition.* Rowley, MA: Newbury House Publishers, 1978.
7. Slavin, Robert. "Research on Cooperative Learning: Consensus and Controversy." *Educational Leadership.* 47. 4 (1990).
8. Zanger, Virginia Vogel. *The Social Context of Second Language Learning: An Examination of Barriers to Integration in Five Case Studies.* Unpublished doctoral dissertation, Boston University, 1987.
9. Zanger, Virginia Vogel. "Social and Cultural Dimensions of the Education of Language Minority Students." Alba Ambert, Ed., *Bilingual Education and English as a Second Language: A Research Handbook, 1988-1990.* New York: Garland Publishing, Inc., 1991.

What Face to Face *is all About*

An American is telling a joke. You feel good because you understand every word.
All of a sudden, everyone is laughing. Everyone except you.

Has this ever happened to you? If you understand all the words, why don't you get the joke? One answer is that words aren't all there is to communication. The fact is that language is not even the most important part of communication: it explains only 35 percent. What, then, explains the rest? The eyes, the face, and the rest of the body all help communicate meaning. These are all parts of body language, or *non-verbal communication. How* the words are spoken is also important. And so is something else: whether the speaker and listener see the world in the same way. Every culture uses different body language, styles of communication, and has different ways of seeing the world. So even if your English grammar is perfect, you will never understand what Americans mean until you know about their non-verbal communication and understand how they think.

Face to Face will help you learn more about these parts of American culture so that you can communicate better with Americans. This is how a student advisor explained it to international students at MIT, a famous American college of technology:

> Sciences can get you 'in' but you need more if you want to go 'up.' Especially the ability to communicate with Americans. It's important to know the system. Americans are born into it. You have to learn it. Your English class is an excellent opportunity.

Face to Face will help you find out some of the ways that Americans are most like people from your own culture, and some of the ways that they are most different. You will also learn about how different Americans are *from each other,* just as people from your background are not all alike.

The book will tell you some things about American culture, but you and your classmates will also find out a lot for yourselves. How? By asking American people to answer questions about the American way of life. You will find these questions in the *Out-of-class Questionnaire* in the middle of each chapter. You will have a chance to practice asking these questions with a partner in class first. That way, you will also find out more about the cultural backgrounds of your classmates.

By the time you finish the chapters in *Face to Face* that your class chooses to cover, you still may not laugh at every American joke you hear. But you *will* understand better why Americans think it is funny.

What is Culture? Some Definitions

Which of the photographs at the right shows a meaning of *culture?*

The answer is all three pictures. Culture is more than just the arts, (a.) or how people live (b.). It is also the way people communicate with each other (c.). *Culture is the total way of life that a group of people share.*

For example, each culture decides:

- how people get married (their customs)
- what parents teach their children about right and wrong (their values)
- how people show respect for each other (their nonverbal communication)
- how schools are organized (their institutions)

a.

b.

c.

THINK ABOUT THIS

- Just as you cannot always see a piece of dirt on the sunglasses that you are wearing, your own culture is often invisible to you.
- Every human being belongs to at least one culture.
- Babies are born without culture; all culture is learned.
- All cultures are constantly changing.

- Most people feel that their own culture is best. This is called *ethnocentrism.*
- In fact, no culture is better or worse than any other culture. A cultural difference does not mean that one culture is right and the other is wrong.
- All people of all cultures have the same basic human needs, such as housing, food, love, and respect. Cultures have different ways of answering these needs.
- Cultural differences can make life both difficult and interesting.

☰ With a Partner

1. Choose one of the statements above which you both believe to be true. Talk about it.
2. Together, list two examples. Take turns giving examples and writing them down.

WHEN YOU STUDY ABOUT DIFFERENT CULTURES...

A Puppy

Animals have four legs. TRUE OR FALSE?

This puppy has four legs. But just because you know that one kind of animal does, you cannot *generalize* that all animals do. (Worms and snakes, for example, have no legs at all.) To say that all animals have four legs is an *overgeneralization.*

When you interview Americans and think about what they say, try not to overgeneralize. Find out what the Americans interviewed by the other students in your class had to say before you make any generalizations.

WARNING: Do not expect Face to Face to be like other textbooks

Here are some ways in which this book is different from other books you may have used in school. Be prepared!

- You will cover only the chapters of greatest interest to your class. Your teacher will decide which chapters and activities will work best for the interests and English language needs of your class. The book was not written to be covered in a semester-long ESL course. But because it is a guide to exploring American culture, after your course is over you can continue to use the book on your own, or with a friend if you can. Choose a chapter that sounds interesting, and read the case study and background reading. Then use the questions on the Out-of-class Questionnaire to interview an American.

- Most of the classwork will be done with a partner, or in a small group with three other students. You will work with a different partner for each chapter. There are several reasons why *Face to Face* has students work together. First, you will have more opportunity to practice speaking English. Second, by working in small groups with your classmates, you will learn about other ways of seeing the world and other cultures, especially if you have classmates from different backgrounds. You will learn more about differences among Americans when your classmates share the information that they learn in their interviews with Americans. Third, your partner will help you with the assignment to interview an American: by interviewing someone together, or by giving you practice in asking the questions, or by talking over what you learned. Finally, it is more fun and also very important to learn to work well in groups. In the workplace at every level, an essential job skill is knowing how to work well with others. In *Face to Face,* there are many activities to help you and your classmates develop this skill.

- For every chapter of *Face to Face* covered by your class, you will spend about half an hour asking an American some questions from the book and taking notes on what you find out. Some students find these interviews an exciting adventure. Almost everyone is a little scared at first. That is why you will work with a partner for your first and perhaps second interview. The book will also give you help: interview tips, questionnaires with questions to ask in your interviews, extra vocabulary words about the interview topic that you might hear in your interview, and a chance to practice asking the questions with a partner in class first. Students who have used *Face to Face* have found that interviewing Americans has helped them in several ways:
  - The practice makes them feel better about speaking English.
  - They get to know some Americans better.
  - They understand how American culture works.
  - They have a chance to share their own culture.

• You will be asked to do some writing which your teacher will *not* correct. In each chapter, there are journal writing asssignments. The goal of this kind of writing is to help you to think about the topic — and what it means in your life — by writing about it. Your teacher may read these journal assignments, but your grammar and spelling will not be corrected. The *ideas* are what is important in journal writing, not the style. There are other writing activities in *Face to Face* that your teacher will correct for grammar, spelling, punctuation, and organization.

What are Your Questions?

From American movies, television, books, and people you may have met, you already know a lot about American culture. But you probably have some questions, too. For example, you may have wondered: *why do Americans...?* Or, you may have noticed someone doing something and want to know: *is that typically American, or just something which that individual person does?* You may have heard something and want to know: *is it really true that Americans...?*

On a separate sheet of paper, *without* writing your name, write down at least two questions that you have about Americans and the American way of life, all the things you would really like to find out about how Americans think and act.

Your teacher will make a list of the class's questions. Discuss them together. This list will help your teacher and the class decide which chapters of *Face to Face* to cover. As you work through the chapters, try to find some answers to these questions.

Chapter 1

Body Language

Warm-up

THINK ABOUT THIS

Gestures are words that are spoken with our hands. The picture on the left shows one of the most common gestures used in the United States.

1. What do Americans mean when they use this gesture?
2. Does it mean the same thing in your native culture?
3. Do you think this gesture means the same thing all over the world?

☰ With a Partner from a Different Language Background (if possible)

1. Talk over your answers with a classmate from a different language background (or a different country) if possible.
2. Show your partner two gestures that are common in your native culture. See if your partner can guess what they mean.
3. Guess the meanings of two gestures that your partner shows you.

JOURNAL

Our bodies tell people a lot about how we feel. In your journal, write about the following:
When you watch people, how do you know if they like you? When people like you, describe:

- how close they stand to you
- how they look at you
- how they touch you — or do not touch you
- the look on their faces

Begin your journal like this:

> *This is how I can tell when people like me. They . . .*

End your journal by copying and completing these sentences:

> *This is how I know when people do not like me. They . . .*

1. _____

   _____

2. _____

   _____

3. _____

   _____

4. _____

   _____

5. _____

_____

6. _____

_____

····················
THINK ABOUT THIS

What do these common American gestures mean?

≡ With a Partner

1. Talk about what the gestures in the photos mean where you come from.
2. Decide what they mean to Americans. On the first line under each picture, write a word or two about what Americans mean when they use the gesture.
3. Talk over whether each gesture is rude, informal, or polite. Then write your choice on the second line under the photograph.
4. Share with your classmates the answers that you and your partner wrote down, and then check them below.

> polite) 6. telephone. (informal)
> (informal) 4. Hi, friend; or I'm joking (informal or rude) 5. I can't hear you. (informal or
> 1. everything is fine; good job. (informal) 2. I hope; let's hope. (informal) 3. come here.

Preparation

CASE STUDY

Susana was slowly combing her hair. Her sister Liliana said to her in Spanish, "Hurry up, Susana, or you'll be late for class again. And isn't today the day that your new American friend, Jane, is coming here to pick you up?" As she spoke, Liliana gestured for her sister to hurry by shaking her hand and letting her fingers snap together.

Susana answered her, "Oh, Liliana. I have writing class today, and I don't feel like going. That American teacher just doesn't like me!"

Liliana frowned and asked, "What happened? Just a month ago you said you liked her so much. How can you tell she doesn't like you?"

"Well, you always know if someone doesn't like you," said Susana. "And though she says nice things to me, I can tell that Mrs. West doesn't really like me. Last week, for example, I asked her a question after class. I noticed that she started moving farther and farther away from me while we talked. And once, when I told her I liked her neck-lace and started to touch it, she jumped away from me like I had some disease! Maybe it's not me. Maybe she's just a cold person."

Before her sister could answer, the doorbell rang, and Susana opened the door. Jane said hi and waved, while Susana kissed her sister good-bye.

Susana and Jane greeted each other with smiles and began walking to class. Jane asked, "So, is your sister going away?"

THINK ABOUT THIS

1. How does Susana feel about Mrs. West?
2. How does Mrs. West feel about Susana?
3. If you were Susana's sister, what would you say to her?
4. Why does Jane think that Susana's sister is going away?

≡ With a Partner Who Speaks Your Native Language

1. With a partner, talk over your ideas on how to answer questions 1-4 above. Decide on the best answer for each one.
2. With help from your partner, write the answer to question 1 on one piece of paper. Then help your partner to write the answer to question 2. Take turns writing the answers to all four questions.

3. Look over the case study together and identify all the gestures used by Susana, Liliana, and Jane. Underline them in your book. Talk about what these gestures mean where you each come from.

THINK ABOUT THIS

People around the world use their fingers for counting. Have you ever noticed that not everyone begins counting on the same finger?

1. Have you ever thought about this before or is it part of your "deep culture"?
2. When you count on your fingers, which finger do you begin with?
3. Do you think your choice has to do with your gender, the customs in your culture, or neither?

☰ Take a Stand

1. With everyone in the class, stand up and raise your hand. Raise the finger that you use for "1" when you count on your fingers.
2. With your hand still raised, get into a group with all your classmates who raised the same finger. Put your hands down.
3. Find out where the other people in your group come from. Look around at the other groups. Talk over in your group the answer to this question: Does culture or gender seem to affect which finger your classmates use to begin counting?
4. Find out if all the groups agreed on the same answer.

BACKGROUND READING

From the information given in the case study, we do not know if Susana's writing teacher likes her or not. But we do know that Susana *thinks* that her teacher does not like her because of her body language. Body language is the way we communicate with our bodies, without using words. Susana reads the body language of her American teacher the way that she would read the body language of another Hispanic. In Latin American cultures, people usually stand closer together and touch each other more (if they are of the same gender) than is the custom in the United States and in Asia. In Susana's culture, standing farther away communicates coldness or dislike, which is what Susana reads from her teacher's nonverbal actions.

It certainly is possible that Mrs. West really does not like Susana. But it is also possible that Susana is *mis*reading her teacher because of different cultural customs about personal space, which is how far apart people stand or sit from each other. In the United States, where independence is very important to individuals, people show respect by giving each other a lot of space (by not standing closer than 18 inches).

Americans also show respect by *not* touching each other very much. For example, in most American families it is not the custom for sisters to kiss each other good-bye every day. They do so only if they will not see each other for a while. That is why when Jane saw Susana giving her sister a kiss, she thought that Liliana was going away. Though many Americans respect each other's personal space by not touching much, some individuals and some cultural groups, such as African Americans and Latinos, do touch more.

Because body language is often as different as verbal language, there are many gestures that mean different things in different cultures. For example, the gesture in the photograph at the beginning of this chapter means *everything's great* or *A-OK* to Americans, as it does to people in many other countries. But in France, it also means *zero,* and in Japan it means *money.* And do not use it in Brazil, Tunisia, or Southern Italy — unless you want to make someone very angry, because it is vulgar.

Although it is natural to believe that everyone communicates nonverbally the same way that we do, it is important to remember the differences in cross-cultural situations. A Brazilian might misunderstand your gesture, for example, if you are not aware of cultural differences. Or you might misunderstand someone else, as Susana perhaps misunderstood her teacher. Like Susana, most of us decide if someone likes us from their body language. We learn to read other people's faces, gestures, voices, and other nonverbal signals before we learn to read books. It is part of our deep culture, which we learn very early. We pay attention to the words we use, but we do not always know what our bodies are saying. Liliana was probably not aware that she frowned, for example. And Mrs. West probably did not notice that she backed away while talking to Susana.

Though we often do not even notice our own body language, scientists believe that it speaks louder than our words. It is believed that 65% of communication happens nonverbally, or without words. Our face, hands, tone of voice, eyes, and other body movements often tell the real story, no matter what our words say. But we may misread the story that is told by someone from another culture, even if we understand the words. One way to learn to correctly read the 65% of communication that happens nonverbally is to be clear about the body language used in our *own* culture. In the next section, the first Questionnaire will let you do just that. The second Questionnaire will give you a chance to learn more about nonverbal communication in the United States.

GLOSSARY FOR BACKGROUND READING VOCABULARY

Communicate (communication) — to tell; to give information

Gender — sex: male or female

Dislike — not like; lack of liking

Nonverbal — without words or language

Misread — to read wrong; not to understand the message correctly

Custom — the common or usual way of doing things

Independence (independent) — separate from others; by oneself

Respect — a good opinion of someone (noun); to treat someone right (verb)

Verbal — with words

Vulgar — not polite, not nice; rude or obscene

Misunderstand — to understand wrong; to get the wrong message

☰ With a Partner

1. Find a sentence in the Background Reading that uses each glossary vocabulary word and read it out loud together. Talk over any of the explanations in the glossary that you do not understand.

2. Several of the words in the glossary have **prefixes,** which are the beginning parts of some words. The prefixes used in some of the words in the glossary mean *not.* The prefixes *non, dis,* and *mis* change words to mean the opposite. For example, *non*verbal means *not verbal.* To *dis*like someone is to *not* like them. The prefix *mis* means *wrong.* To *mis*understand something is to understand something wrong. With your partner, figure out the meanings of these words and write them down on one piece of paper:

non	**dis**	**mis**
nonviolent	disrespect	misplace
nonfiction	discontinue	mispronounce
nonresident	dissimilar	misguided
nontoxic	disagree	misuse

THINK ABOUT THIS

What does a person communicate by nodding his or her head up and down?

    a. Yes, I agree with you.
    b. Yes, I'm listening.
    c. Something else.

≡ With a Partner

1. Talk over your answer.
2. Most people from the dominant American culture would choose *a*. Many Asians would choose *b*. Talk about how this cultural difference could be a problem.
3. Together, practice the American custom for showing "Yes, I'm listening." Americans do this by saying "Uh-huh," "Mmm-hmmm," "Really?" or "Yeah" during tiny pauses in the conversation. Practice doing this while your partner tells you about a vacation he or she would like to take someday. Then let your partner practice how to show listening American-style while you talk about a dream vacation.
4. Are you aware of the body language that you use to show that you are listening? This is very much a part of deep culture and something that most people never think about. Show your partner how people in your native culture communicate that they are listening.

Interviews and Analysis

 INTERVIEW TIP: LOOK YOUR INFORMANT IN THE EYE

To fill out Questionnaire 2 in this section, you and a partner will ask questions of an American. This person will be your *informant,* someone who will give you information about American body language. It is natural to feel a little bit scared or nervous about this, especially if it is your first time interviewing an American. The American you interview may feel a little nervous and uncomfortable as well, at least at the beginning.

One thing that you can do to feel less nervous yourself is to practice asking the questions before your interview. One thing that you can do to help your American informant feel more comfortable is to use body language that he or she is used to. When Americans are talking, they feel better if the person they are talking with is looking them straight in the eye. When you make eye contact this way, Americans feel that you are listening to them. If you look your American informant in the eye during your interview, he or she will feel that it is more like a natural conversation and will probably give you better answers.

Because in many other cultures people do not have the same custom of looking directly at others during conversation, it may take some practice for you to get used to doing it comfortably.

≡ Practice with a Partner

1. Read the following dialogue over twice by yourself.
2. Turn to the classmate sitting next to you and read it together out loud. Take turns reading each part.
3. Put your books down, stand up, and practice saying the dialogue while looking each other in the eye. You do not have to say the dialogue using the exact same words. The important thing is to get the ideas across while maintaining eye contact.

STUDENT: HEY, JOE, HOW ARE YOU DOING?

JOE AMERICAN: NOT TOO BAD. WHAT'S HAPPENING?

STUDENT: I HAVE A HOMEWORK ASSIGNMENT TO INTERVIEW AN AMERICAN. I WONDER IF YOU COULD HELP ME OUT.

JOE AMERICAN: I DON'T KNOW. I'M KIND OF BUSY. WHAT'S IT ABOUT ANYWAY?

STUDENT: IT'S ABOUT BODY LANGUAGE — GESTURES, PERSONAL SPACE, STUFF LIKE THAT.

JOE AMERICAN: SOUNDS INTERESTING, BUT I'M NO EXPERT.

STUDENT: YOU DON'T HAVE TO BE. JUST SAY WHAT YOU THINK.

JOE AMERICAN: HOW MUCH TIME WOULD IT BE?

STUDENT: Not more than 20 minutes. We could do it now, or whenever is a good time for you. I'd really appreciate it.

JOE AMERICAN: Well, I guess I have a little time now.

STUDENT: Thanks a million. Hold on while I get the questions.

Note: When you interview someone, you will find it hard to look your informant in the eye *and* take notes about what he or she says at the same time. It will be a lot easier if you have some help. Using Questionnaire 2, you will work with a partner to interview an American about body language. You and your partner can take turns asking questions and taking notes. Right after the interview, while the information is still fresh in your minds, go over your notes with your partner and together write down everything else that you remember from the interview.

Questionnaire 1: In-class

BODY LANGUAGE

1. *Find an interview partner among your classmates.*
2. *Exchange names and native countries with your partner.*
3. *Interview each other with Questionnaire 1 below. Take turns asking each other the following questions and answering them. You do not need to take any notes. Remember to practice maintaining eye contact.*

---

1. In your native culture, what gestures, if any, do you use to communicate the following:

   Someone is crazy
   Money
   I don't know
   Good luck
   Come here
   Thank you
   That you want a waiter's attention (in a restaurant)

2. Show me some common *hand* gestures that people from your culture use. Some *arm* gestures. Some *facial* gestures.

3. Are there any gestures that you have seen Americans use that you do not understand?

4. If you see someone smiling, what does it usually mean? What else can it mean, in your culture?

5. What do you communicate if you look directly at older people when they are speaking to you? Can you explain other cultural "rules" for when it is important — or not OK — to look at other people?

6. Do you think it is normal for friends of the same sex to touch? When and how? To hold hands? When is it OK for people of the opposite sex to hold hands?

7. How do you feel when someone stands very close to you (closer than 1 foot or 30 centimeters)? What about very far away (more than 3 feet or 1 meter) while you are talking?

8. If you go to a job interview, what is the correct body language to use when you are introduced to the boss?

9. Show me the body language that you would see in a normal, everyday greeting between:

   a. two male coworkers
   b. two female friends
   c. male and female friends
   d. members of your family

10. Does everyone from your country greet each other according to the same customs? Explain.

11. Has it been hard for you to get used to American body language in any way? Explain.

☰ With Your Interview Partner

1. After you have finished interviewing each other, talk over how your answers to the questions were different in any way.

2. Write down both of your answers to questions 3 and 11 on one piece of paper and give it to your teacher.

3. Together, think up one extra question of your own about American body language that you would like to ask the American you interview. Write it down in the space after question 11 on Questionnaire 2.

4. When you interview an American later on with Questionnaire 2, you will ask if he or she understands a gesture from your culture. Ask your partner to help you choose one, and note it on Questionnaire 2, question 3.

5. Plan the interview that you and your interview partner will do with an American informant. Decide on possible times for both of you, and who you could ask. If you need to talk about it more after class, give each other your telephone number.

Questionnaire 2: Out-of-class

BODY LANGUAGE IN THE UNITED STATES

With your interview partner, ask an American informant the following questions. Ask some of the questions yourself while your partner takes notes. Then switch, and take notes while your partner asks the questions. Do not read the instructions in parentheses () out loud.

Before the interview: *Read over the questions out loud to yourself and then to your partner. Make a note about which gestures from your cultures you and your partner will ask your informant. Write them down in the space after question 3 below. Add a question of your own in the space after question 11.*

After the interview: *Ask your American informant to sign his or her name. Thank him or her. In the space at the end, write down any new vocabulary you hear or learn during the interview. Go over all the questions and notes with your partner and make your notes more complete.*

1. What gestures, if any, do you use to communicate:

   Someone is crazy _____

   Money _____

   I don't know _____

   Good luck _____

   Come here _____

   Thank you _____

   That you want a waiter's attention _____

   (Put a check ✓ next to each gesture that means the *same* thing as the gesture when it is used in your culture.)

2. Could you show me some other common American gestures and tell me what they mean?

   _____

   _____

3. Could you tell me what this gesture means to you? (Show a gesture from your native culture.)

   _____

4. If you see someone smiling, what does it usually mean? What else can it mean?

_____

_____

5. What do you communicate if you look directly at older people when they are speaking to you? Can you explain any other "rules" for when it is important — or not OK —to look directly at other people?

_____

_____

6. Do you think it is normal for friends of the same sex to touch? When and how? What about holding hands? When is it OK for people of the opposite sex to hold hands?

_____

_____

_____

7. How do you feel when someone stands very close to you — less than a foot away? How close is too close? Could you show me? How do you feel when someone stands back, say three feet, while you are talking? When talking to a friend, how close do you like to stand? Show me.

_____

_____

_____

_____

8. If you go to a job interview, what is the correct body language to use when you are introduced to the boss? What should you say?

_____

_____

9. Describe or show me the body language that you would see in a normal, every-day greeting between:

    a. two American male coworkers _____

    b. two female friends _____

    c. male and female friends _____

    d. members of your family _____

10. Would you say that most Americans use the same greetings? Explain.

    _____

    _____

11. Your own question.

    _____

    _____

Signature of American informant: _____ Date: _____

Partner's signature: _____

How do you know the informant? _____

New vocabulary: _____

ANALYSIS WITH YOUR INTERVIEW PARTNER

Get together with your interview partner and talk over the interview that you did with an American informant. Ask each other the following questions. After you both answer, write a checkmark next to the question.

___1. How did you each feel before the interview? During the interview? After the interview?
___2. How clearly did you ask the questions? Did you maintain eye contact?

__3. Did your partner help you? How?

__4. What will you try to remember to do the next time you have to interview an American?

__5. Show the American gestures that your informant showed you when he or she answered questions 1, 2, and 3. Choose one that was new to you and practice it. Be ready to perform it for the whole class.

__6. Stand up and do the four greetings that your American informant showed you in question 9. Choose one and practice it so that you can do it for the whole class. Together, look over the notes that you and your partner took during the interview with your American informant. On one piece of paper, take turns writing down the answers to these questions:

__7. What new information about American culture did you learn from the interview?

__8. Write down any answers that you did not understand.

__9. Think about your American informant's answers to questions 1-9, and how you and your partner each answered these questions on Questionnaire 1. Fill in the chart below by writing the question numbers:

Questions that the three of you answered the same	Questions that two of you answered the same	Questions that you all answered differently

10. Think about how you and you partner answered questions 3-7. Based on that information, write some "rules" about what to do when talking with Americans in the space below.

RULES FOR BODY LANGUAGE IN THE U.S.

Smiling (question 4).
Examples: *Smile when you are happy. Don't smile when you are nervous.*

Eye contact (question 5).
Example: *Teach your children to look adults in the eye.*

Touching (question 6).
Example: *If you are male, it is all right to slap a male friend on the back to show friendship.*

Personal space (question 7).
Example: *If you stand closer than 12 inches, Americans will think that you are pushy.*

ANALYSIS IN CLASS

1. Talk over with your classmates how your interview with an American went. Discuss how you and your classmates found someone to interview. Tell one thing that you and your partner will try to remember for your next interview.
2. Share one American gesture with your classmates that you and your partner learned. Watch as someone from each pair shows the American gesture that they learned.
3. On the board, write down some of the "rules" that you and your partner learned about American body language. Other pairs will do the same. Organize your rules into these categories on the board:
   - Smiling
   - Eye contact
   - Touching
   - Personal space

   Talk over the rules on the blackboard, especially if there are any that seem to conflict with each other.

4. Share with your classmates how these rules may be similar or different from body language in your culture. Listen as your classmates talk about the customs of their native country. Based on this discussion, write down one rule for each category from other cultures represented in the class (not your native culture). After each rule, identify which culture it comes from.

RULES FOR BODY LANGUAGE AROUND THE WORLD

Smiling

Example: *Smile when you are embarrassed about something (Japan).*

Eye contact

Touching

Personal space

---

5. Stand up with your partner and show the class one American greeting. Do not tell them the genders or the relationship of the greeters (two males, two family members, etc.) and see if your classmates can guess. Then watch as other pairs perform an American greeting and try to guess who is doing the greeting.

6. Tell the class the extra question that you and your partner asked your American informant (question 11). Share the answer you learned. Listen to what the other pairs found out.

7. Your teacher will read a list of what confuses or bothers you and your classmates about American body language (what each pair wrote in response to question 11 on Questionnaire 1). Discuss these together. Talk over any answers that American informants gave that were confusing or hard to understand.

JOURNAL

While you are still learning English, you may have to use even more nonverbal communication than you do in your own language. What did you find out about American body language through the work you did in this chapter? How will this information help you to communicate better with Americans? What is still hard for you to get used to doing in American body language?

AMERICAN PERSONAL DISTANCE CATEGORIES (4) WHEN TALKING

CATEGORY	1. INTIMATE	2. PERSONAL	3. SOCIAL	4. PUBLIC
How Far: (feet)	0 - 1½	1½ - 4	4 - 12	12 →
(cm)	0 - 45	45 - 120	120 - 365	365 →
Voice	whisper or very soft	low volume	full voice	loud voice
Who	lovers, parents of small children	friends relatives acquaintances	business relationships	performers speakers etc.
What	intimate, secrets	personal, confidential	business	formal presentation

THINK ABOUT THIS

The four categories in the chart above show how far apart Americans are used to standing from each other in different situations. For example, when Americans stand 5 inches, 10 inches, or 15 inches apart from each other, they are in an intimate situation, talking with a lover in a whisper, about intimate or very personal things. This category is known as *intimate space*.

Americans feel comfortable talking to friends in a soft voice at a distance of 18 inches, 2 feet, or even 4 feet about personal matters within this *personal space*. In business relationships, Americans stand from 4 to 12 feet apart and speak in a full voice. This is *social space*. Finally, *public space,* a distance of 12 feet or greater, is used in more formal situations, such as formal talks or presentations. Using the information from this chart, answer:

How far away do Americans stand in these situations:

1. When giving a speech?
2. When talking to a clerk in a store?
3. When asking a stranger for directions?
4. When talking to their cousins?
5. When telling a friend a story?

≡ With a Partner from the Same Part of the World

1. Go over your answers to the questions together. If you have trouble, ask another pair for help.
2. Talk over how you would answer the same questions yourselves. At what distance would you feel comfortable in each situation? Do these cultural differences help explain why people from some cultures are said to be cold and distant?
3. Stand up and practice having a conversation in each of the four American categories. Talk with your partner for 45 seconds about what happened on the way to school today while standing:

   a. 4 feet (120 cm) apart
   b. 1 1/2 feet (45 cm) apart
   c. 1 foot (30 cm) apart

   Talk over how you both felt at each distance.

Additional Activities

DIALOGUE

With a partner, read the following dialogue*. It is a conversation between two friends: One is healthy and one has laryngitis and cannot speak. Read the part of "Healthy Student" while your partner answers with gestures from his or her cultural background. Add extra lines and gestures if you can. Then switch roles. Finally, practice playing the part of the student with laryngitis, using American body language. As you go through each version of the dialogue, make sure to include a nonverbal farewell that is typical of the culture you are showing.

HEALTHY STUDENT: ARE YOU FEELING ANY BETTER?

STUDENT WITH LARYNGITIS: (GESTURES ANSWER)

HEALTHY STUDENT: WELL, I HOPE YOU'RE OVER THIS COLD BEFORE YOUR COUSIN'S PARTY THIS WEEKEND. WHAT WAS HER LAST PARTY LIKE?

STUDENT WITH LARYNGITIS: (GESTURES ANSWER)

HEALTHY STUDENT: I HEARD THERE WAS A LOT OF FOOD. HOW WAS IT?

STUDENT WITH LARYNGITIS: (GESTURES ANSWER)

HEALTHY STUDENT: I BELIEVE IT! WELL, I HAVE TO GO STUDY FOR TOMORROW'S EXAM. I'M REALLY UPTIGHT ABOUT IT.

STUDENT WITH LARYNGITIS: (GESTURES "GOOD LUCK")

HEALTHY STUDENT: THANKS. TAKE CARE NOW. BYE.

(BOTH STUDENTS GESTURE FAREWELL.)

   * The idea for this dialogue was inspired by a dialogue in *Teacher Training Pack for a Course on Cultural Awareness* by Carmen Judith Nine Curt.

OUTLINING ASSIGNMENT

Write an outline to help you organize your ideas for writing a paper on the following topic: "What would an American visitor to your native country need to know about nonverbal communication there?"

1. If possible, get together with a classmate who comes from the same part of the world. Together, brainstorm a list of all of the typical body language that people there use when they communicate with each other. Take notes.

2. Use your notes to make an outline of the information. Use the following form as a guide, filling in the blank spaces with information from your notes.
3. Show your outline to your partner and ask if all the information from your brainstorming discussion is included in your outline. Check over your partner's outline.

NONVERBAL COMMUNICATION IN _____ CULTURE

I. Gestures
   A. Common gestures
      1.
      2.
      3.
      4.
   B. Gestures NOT to use
      1.
      2.
      3.
      4.

II. Eye Contact
   A. To show respect
      1.
      2.
      3.
      4.
   B. To communicate other things
      1.
      2.

III. Personal Space
   A. When talking to each other, most people stand _____
      1.
      2.
   B. Sometimes people stand _____
      1.
      2.

IV. Greetings
   A. Meeting people for the first time
      1.
      2.
      3.
      4.

B. How friends greet each other
   1.
   2.
   3.
C. Greeting an older person
   1.
   2.
   3.
V. Other Things to Know
  A.
  B.
  C.

Follow-Up Writing Assignment: If you did an outline like the one above, use it to write a composition or essay about body language in your native culture. Start a new paragraph for each part that begins with a Roman numeral (such as I, II, or IV). Begin each paragraph with a topic sentence about what is written next to each Roman numeral or capital letter in your outline.

Example: Begin a paragraph based on Roman numeral V in the outline above with this topic sentence: *There are also several other important things to know about the body language that is used in my native country.*

Chapter 2

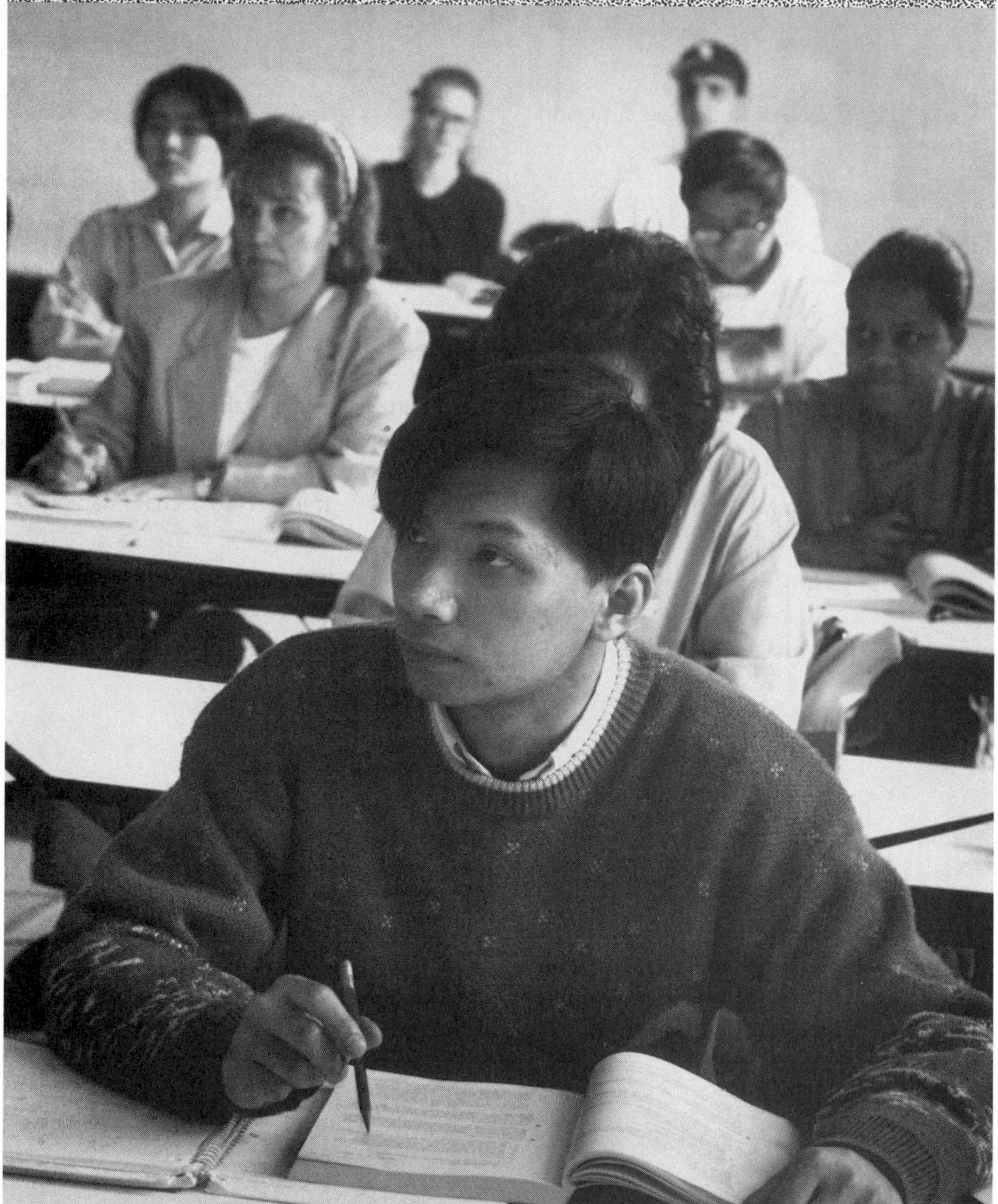

Warm-up

THINK ABOUT THIS

People are in school for many different reasons.

1. What are some reasons why school is important to you?
2. Make a list of at least four reasons. Underline the reason that is most important to you.

≡ With a Partner

1. Compare your lists. Talk about why you each chose the reason that you underlined.
2. Together, think of ten reasons why school is important for everyone and take turns writing them down.
3. Organize the list into categories. *Examples:* children, immigrants, money, etc.
4. Write the names of your categories on the board. The other pairs of classmates will do the same. Did everyone think about this issue in the same way?

JOURNAL

Are your memories of school when you were a child mostly good or mostly bad? Explain, describing some specific experiences that you remember. Now that you are older, how is your school experience different?

Preparation

CASE STUDY

Taro had studied English for many years in Japan. Yet he was afraid that language would be a big problem for him in his classes at an American university. He was glad to find out that he was able to understand most of the readings for his class, The Modern American Novel, though he had to spend a long time on each one. Understanding the class discussions was harder, as Taro knew it would be. But what surprised Taro was the difficulty that he had in understanding what was going on between the other students and the professor.

It began on the first day of his class on American novels. When he walked in, four or five students were drinking from cans of soda. When the professor began teaching, they continued drinking. Dr. Gomez, the professor, did not seem to mind. He sat right down on top of a desk and said,

"Good morning, I'm Alan Gomez. Feel free to call me Alan — or Professor Gomez if you prefer."

Taro knew that Americans often called each other by their first name. Still, it was hard for him to think of calling a professor "Alan."

Then the professor gave the class a list of the novels to be read for the semester. Lisa, a student in the back of the classroom, raised her hand to ask a question.

"Professor Gomez, I noticed that this list doesn't have any novels written by Alice Walker. I'm very interested in her work. Would it be all right with you if I read a couple of her novels instead of some of the readings that are on this list?"

Taro was surprised by the student's question, but Dr. Gomez did not seem to be. He told the student to see him after class to talk about it. Then he asked if there were any more questions.

☰ Talk Over with a Partner

1. What surprised Taro on the first day of class?
2. Why do you think he was surprised?
3. What about Dr. Gomez' first class is similar to your experiences with American teachers or professors? Write your answer to question 3 on the board while other pairs do the same. Discuss them together.

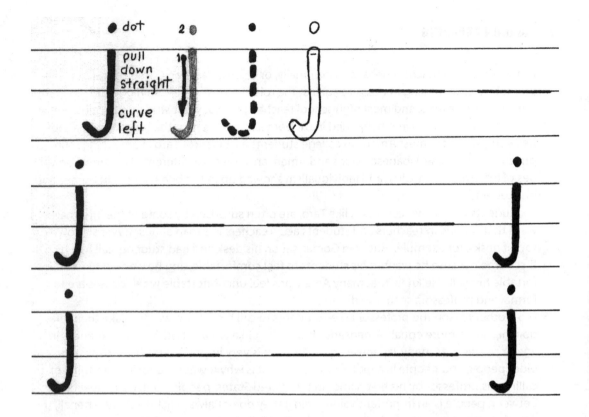

·····················
THINK ABOUT THIS

In the United States, it is estimated that one out of every four adults cannot read or write well enough to fill out a job application; they are *illiterate*. There are now a number of literacy programs in many towns and cities to teach illiterate adults how to read and write.

Is illiteracy a problem where you come from?

☰ Take Sides

1. Raise your hand if you answered *yes* to the question above.
2. If more than three students answered *yes,* go to one side of the room with everyone else who answered *yes.* Classmates who answered *no* will go stand on the other side of the room.
3. Discuss why so many people in your countries do not (or do) learn to read.
4. As a group, make a list of suggestions about what countries can do to improve their literacy rates.

BACKGROUND READING

Not all American teachers behave as informally, or casually, as Alan Gomez did. For example, eating and drinking in class are against the rules in most American high schools. Many university professors, and most high school teachers, do not want students to call them by their first names. But what happened in Dr. Gomez' classroom on the first day would not be as surprising for most American college students as it was for Taro. Some things surprised Taro because Japanese values and American values are different. The American values of informality, equality, and individualism showed up in the behavior of Dr. Gomez and his students.

Students from other countries, like Taro, are often surprised by some of the informal ways that American teachers and students act. Teachers in Japan almost never sit down on top of desks, for example. But Alan Gomez sat on his desk and had students call him by his first name because he wanted his students to feel comfortable, and he wanted to feel comfortable himself. He knew that many Americans feel uncomfortable when classes are too formal and professors seem too distant.

Another reason the professor asked students to call him "Alan" was to make their relationship seem more equal. Americans often do not like to call attention to differences in age or position, as many Japanese do. In Japan, it is very important to show respect for older people and people in a higher position. That is why it was hard for Taro to think of calling his professor by his first name. In the United States, people think that equality between people is an important value, even if they do not always act that way. After all, the American government was built on the idea that "all men are created equal."

Taro was also surprised by Lisa asking if she could read something different from what the professor had planned. In American culture, the individual is more important than the group, and so individuals try to do what they think is best for them as individuals. "Do your own thing" is a popular way of expressing this idea of individualism. Because of this idea, Professor Gomez was not surprised that his student felt free to ask about making such a change.

It is even possible that Lisa's question made Dr. Gomez think more highly of her. Because individualism is so important in American life, teachers believe that it is important for students to have their own ideas about what is being studied, and Lisa's question showed Dr. Gomez that she did. In American classrooms, it is not enough for students to show that they read and understand what is in their books. Saying what they think about what they've read is just as important. In fact, many teachers give students grades for class participation (how much they talk and ask intelligent questions during class discussions).

GLOSSARY FOR BACKGROUND READING VOCABULARY

Behave — to act
Equality — the idea that people should be treated the same way; that differences in age, money, and power should not matter
Individualism — the idea that the person, or individual, is more important than the group
Informality — the idea that things should be friendly and casual, not formal

Participation — taking part in or joining in, usually shown by talking

Position — a person's place in a group, or level in society; often used to describe how much money or power someone has

Relationship — connection; what people mean to each other and how they interact with each other

Values — what is most important to people; how people think that they and others should act; the way that people think the world should be

≡ With a Partner

1. Talk over whether you have had any surprises like Taro's about how classes are run in the United States.
2. According to the reading, what American values help explain what went on in Taro's classroom?
3. Take turns answering the questions in the following vocabulary exercise.

Noun	Verb	Adjective
relationship	relate	participating
relative	behave, behaves	formal
behavior	participating	informal
participation	participate	valuable
informality	individualize	
individual	value	
individualism		
values		

The eight words in the Chapter 2 glossary also have other grammatical forms. Read each sentence below and choose the correct grammatical form of the words in parentheses to fill in the blank.

Example: Lisa's question showed that she was not afraid to ___*relate*___ to her professor as an equal. (relationship, relative, relate)

1. Taro had read that Americans are more informal than the Japanese, but he was still surprised by the _____ of the students in his class. (behave, behaves, behavior)
2. Out of respect, students in Japan do not often ask questions of their teachers; thus, it may be hard at first for Japanese students to _____ in American classroom discussions. (participate, participating, participation)
3. American students love casual clothes like blue jeans, but at big dances _____ clothes are more typical. (informality, informal, formal)
4. Most American children wear clothes they like to school, not uniforms; this may be another way that schools teach the value of _____ . (individual, individualize, individualism)
5. Though American and Japanese cultures both _____ education, their forms of schooling are different. (valuable, values, value)

······················
THINK ABOUT THIS

Many American public schools have bilingual education programs for students whose first language is not English. Students study subjects in their native language while they also study English.

1. What do you think about bilingual programs in American schools?
2. Are there bilingual schools in your native country? What languages are taught? Who studies there? Why?
3. Have you ever studied in another language before?

☰ With a Partner

1. Compare your answers to the questions above.
2. Many Americans do not understand the advantages of being bilingual. Together, brainstorm a list of reasons why it is better to be bilingual. Write it down.
3. If you could design a school to send your children to that would ensure that they could read, write, and speak two languages, what would it be like? With your partner, write a typical course schedule for students in the second grade and one for students in high school.

Interviews and Analysis

 INTERVIEW TIP: FOLLOW-UP QUESTIONS

The goal of doing an interview with an American informant is to understand an *insider's* point of view on American culture. Therefore, the more your informant explains his or her answers, the better. In a good interview, most of the talking is done by the person you interview, not by you.

How can you get your informant to give you more information or explain an answer better? Before asking the next question on the questionnaire, ask a follow-up question. It is best if you make up follow-up questions that do not have simple yes-or-no answers. Here are some examples of follow-up questions that require an informant to talk in more detail:

1. "Could you tell me more about that?"
2. "Could you give me an example of that?"
3. "Explain a little more about what you mean by that."
4. "If I was to go there, what would I see?" (for some questions)
5. "Tell me what a typical _____ is like." (for some questions)

≡ Practice with a Partner

Take turns interviewing each other, asking "What is your favorite subject in school?" Use at least three follow-up questions each to find out more information about each other's ideas.

Interview Vocabulary

Review the meanings of the following words, which will come up in your interviews:

1. *To cheat* — to copy
2. *To drop out* — to leave before graduating
3. *Extracurricular* — after class, voluntary
4. *Former* — earlier, previous, last
5. *Quotation marks* — Punctuation (") showing someone is speaking.

Questionnaire 1: In-class

SCHOOLS IN OTHER COUNTRIES

Choose an interview partner in your class who:

- *feels the way you do about learning English (ask your classmates)*
- *comes from a different country than you — if possible*

Interview your partner about his or her experiences in school, using the following questions as a beginning. Ask at least four follow-up questions. Your partner will also interview you. You do not need to take notes.

1. What school did you last attend in your native country? Did you choose it? If so, why?
2. What did you study? Why did you take those courses?
3. What extracurricular activities were you part of there? What did you like about them?
4. In your old school, what did you do if you did not understand something in one of your classes?
5. What did you do if a teacher gave you a grade that you did not think was fair?
6. Where you come from, what do teachers think about students asking questions in class? What do teachers think about students who never ask questions?
7. In your former school, if you did not agree with what a teacher said, would you ever say so? What would a teacher think if you did say something? What would other students think?
8. In your culture, how do students show that they are paying attention?
9. Where you come from, do many students drop out of school? What do you think are their reasons?
10. How often do students cheat in your country? How do most students feel about it?
11. Imagine that a student hands in an excellent term paper, but it has some sentences and paragraphs copied from another book without quotation marks or the author's name. In your old school, would there be a problem if the teacher found out that some of it was copied? What would happen?
12. What, do you think, is the hardest thing for international students at American schools to get used to?

Signature of interview partner: _____

Native country: _____

☰ Pair Work

1. After you and your interview partner have interviewed each other, think about which questions you answered the same and which you answered differently. To see these similarities and differences more clearly, fill in the Venn diagram below together:

Directions for Venn Diagram. In the middle, where the two circles meet, write the answers that you and your partner gave that were similar. In the half-circles on either side, write the answers that are different in your native country and in your partner's.
Example: If you and your partner both answered question 5 with "ask a friend after class," you will write that in the middle, where the two circles meet. If you answer "ask a friend," but your informant answers "get help from the teacher after class," do not write anything in the middle. Instead, write each answer on either side of where the two circles meet.

Schooling

In _____ (country)   In both countries   In _____ (country)

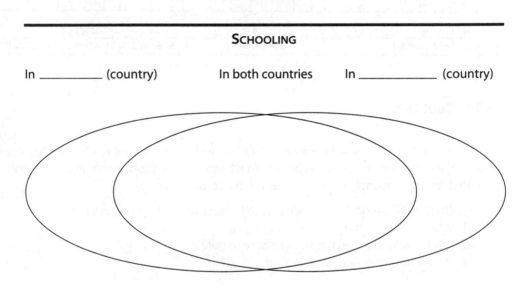

2. You and your partner will interview an American informant together about School in the U.S., using Questionnaire 2. Make a plan about who you can ask and where and when the interview should take place. Decide which one of you will begin asking questions while the other takes notes, and when you will switch. Then prepare for the interview by deciding on one extra question that you will each ask your informant. Write them in the spaces next to questions 13 and 14 on Questionnaire 2.

City University
OFFICE OF THE UNIVERSITY REGISTRAR
DROP/ADD FORM

YOUR COLLEGE OF REGISTRATION
|S|E|D|

ID/SOCIAL SECURITY NUMBER
|6|8|3|4|2|2|1|9|8|

|M|E|N|D|O|S|A|,| |C|A|R|L|O|S| | | | | | | | |

CALENDAR YEAR 19 |9,3|

SEMESTER (circle one)
(FALL) SPRING SUM I SUM II

ACTION circle one	COLLEGE OF COURSE	COURSE NUMBER	SEC-TION	CREDIT HOURS	AU NC	EFFECTIVE DATE Month Day Year			ADM	INSTRUCTOR SIGNATURE
Add (Drop)	S,E,D	P,h,1,0,2	C,2	4.0		,9	2,0	9,3	,	P.Celeesn
(Add) Drop	S,E,D	C,h,2,1,1	B,4	4.0		,9	2,0	9,3	,	R.Row
Add Drop		, , ,	,	,		,	,	,	,	

CREDIT CHANGES FOR VARIABLE CREDIT COURSES ONLY

ACTION	COLLEGE OF COURSE	COURSE NUMBER	SEC-TION	CREDIT HOURS	AU NC	EFFECTIVE DATE Month Day Year			ADM	INSTRUCTOR SIGNATURE
Cr. Ch		, , ,	,	,		,	,	,	,	

Carlos Mendosa   9/20/93   *H.Gaulaway*
Student Signature   Date   ADVISOR'S SIGNATURE (IF REQUIRED)

....

THINK ABOUT THIS

This is a form used at one American college for students who want to change their course schedule after the semester has begun. Most American schools are somewhat flexible about letting students change courses up to a certain date.

1. On this Drop/Add form, which course is the student changing *out of?*
2. Which course is the student changing *into?*
3. Whose signature did the student have to get?
4. Is a similar procedure used at your school?

≡ With a Partner

1. Compare answers to the questions above. Together, write down what a student at your school has to do to change courses.
2. Sometimes a professor or advisor requires that you give a good reason for changing courses. Write a list of good reasons.
3. Have you ever tried to change out of a course? Talk it over.
4. Talk about how schools in your native country deal with students who want to change courses. Write it down.

≡ With Another Pair of Partners

1. Get together with another pair. Read to each other your answers for questions 1, 2, and 3 above.

Questionnaire 2: Out-of-class

SCHOOLS IN THE U.S.

With your interview partner, interview an American student with the following questions, including some questions of your own at the end. Remember to ask follow-up questions for more complete answers. Write down any new vocabulary you hear or learn during the interview.

1. What school do you attend? Did you choose it? If so, why?

   _____

   _____

2. What are you studying? Why are you taking those courses?

   _____

   _____

3. Are you in any extracurricular activities? What do you like about them?

   _____

   _____

4. What do you do when you do not understand something in one of your classes?

   _____

5. What do you do when a teacher gives you a grade that you do not think is fair?

   _____

6. What do your teachers think about students asking questions in class? What do they think about students who never ask questions?

   _____

   _____

   _____

7. If you do not agree with something that a teacher says, do you ever say so? What do teachers think if you say something? What do other students think when a student questions something the teacher says?

_____

_____

_____

8. How do American students show that they are paying attention?

_____

_____

9. Do many students drop out of your school? What do you think are their reasons?

_____

_____

10. How often do you think students cheat in your classes? What do most students think about cheating?

_____

_____

11. Imagine that a student hands in an excellent term paper, but it has some sentences and paragraphs copied from another book without quotation marks or the author's name. Will there be a problem if the teacher finds out? What will happen?

_____

_____

12. What, do you think, is the hardest adjustment for international students at your school?

_____

_____

13. Your own question.

_____

_____

14. Your own question.

_____

_____

Signature of American informant: _____

Date: _____

New vocabulary: _____

....

ANALYSIS ON YOUR OWN

Look over the answers of the American you interviewed, and fill in a Venn diagram to show the similarities and the differences among schools in the United States and in your native country.

SCHOOLING

In your native country   In the U.S.

In both countries

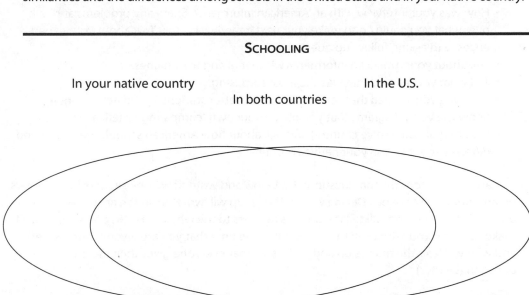

....
ANALYSIS IN PAIRS

Talk over these questions with your interview partner:
1. How did you feel about the interview and how it went?
2. Did you ask follow-up questions and did they help?
3. What surprised you about what the American informant said?
4. Were there any answers that you did not understand?
5. Which of the answers showed how the American values of informality, equality, or individualism are important in American education?

> *Example:* If the answer to question 1 had a lot of information about choosing schools and courses, this may show the American value of individualism. Fill in this chart with the question numbers that relate to each value:

Informality	Equality	Individualism

....
ANALYSIS IN A SMALL GROUP

Part I. You and your partner will meet with another pair of interview partners. Bring along your interview notes and your Venn diagrams. First, take turns telling about your interviews by asking each other the following questions. You do not need to write down answers.

- How was your interview with an American informant? Share any problems and talk over what you could do to make your next interview better. Talk about your experiences with asking follow-up questions.
- Tell about your American informants without giving their names.
- Tell what you learned that was the most surprising.
- Tell what you learned that can help you be a better student in American schools.
- Show the Venn diagrams that you did on your own (comparing American schooling with that of your native country) and talk about how American schools are similar and different to schools in your native country.

Part II. Work together on questions 1-6 below and write down one set of group answers on another piece of paper. Decide who in the group will write down the answers for the group **(Recorder)**, who will tell the group's answers to the whole class **(Reporter)**, who will make sure that you answer all the questions in the time that you are given **(Timekeeper)**, and who will lead the discussion and make sure that everyone gives their ideas on each question **(Leader)**.

☰ Analysis Questions for Small Groups

1. Based on the answers from the American informants who were interviewed, make up and write a one-sentence answer for each of the Interview Questions 4-12, from an American point of view. Begin each sentence with: "In American schools..."

   Example: Question 4: "In American schools, students who do not understand something in class ask their teacher about it or call a friend."

2. Write one or more American answers that show how important the American values of *informality, individualism,* and *equality* are in American schooling.
3. List three things that everyone in the group likes about American schooling. Make sure everyone agrees.
4. Discuss whether your American informants understood the problems of students from other countries (question 11). Write a list of three things that could help American students to understand international students better.
5. Write down any answers given by American informants that you do not understand, after discussing them in the group.
6. How well did your group work together? Write down a number from 1 to 10 (10 is high). _____ List two things that were good and list two things that the group could do to make things even better the next time.

ANALYSIS IN CLASS

The reporters from each small group will tell the class:

1. How did the interviews go? Were there any problems? Did people enjoy them? Did the follow-up questions work?
2. How did each small group answer questions 1-4 above?
3. How did your American respondents answer the extra question that you made up (question 13 or 14, "your own question")?
4. What answers given by American informants were not clear?
5. The whole class will discuss: What are some of the ways that international students may have to change in order to be successful in American schools? Decide how to practice making those changes. Role-play some situations to practice new behaviors.

JOURNAL

Write about what it was like for you to work in the small group with your classmates to analyze the information you got in your interview. What more did you learn about American schools from talking things over with another pair? Based on this experience, what do you think is important for small groups to remember to do in order to work together well?

....
THINK ABOUT THIS

If you were the head of your school, what would you do to make it a better place for students from your background?

≡ With a Partner

1. Make a list of things that your school could do.
2. Talk over how the foreign students at your school could work to get some of these things done.

Additional Activities

ADDITIONAL INTERVIEWS: HOW AMERICAN SCHOOLS HAVE CHANGED

Find out about how American schools have changed since your teachers were students. Using some of the questions from Questionnaire 2, ask one or more of your teachers to tell you about what it was like when they were in school and ask them to talk about the changes that they have seen. Or, ask another adult to be your informant. Compare their answers to what your first American informant told you and to what you have experienced yourself. Write or present an oral report on changes in American schooling.

LETTER FROM YOUR GRANDCHILD: SCHOOL IN THE YEAR 2025

The world is changing, and many people feel that schools will need to change to keep up. Choose a partner, and together imagine that it is the year 2025. Make a list of the ways the world may be different then. Then write down some ways in which schools may be different in response to these changes. Use these ideas to write a letter from a student in the year 2025, telling a grandparent about his or her first day of school. Begin it like this:

Dear Grandma,

   Today was our first day back at school.

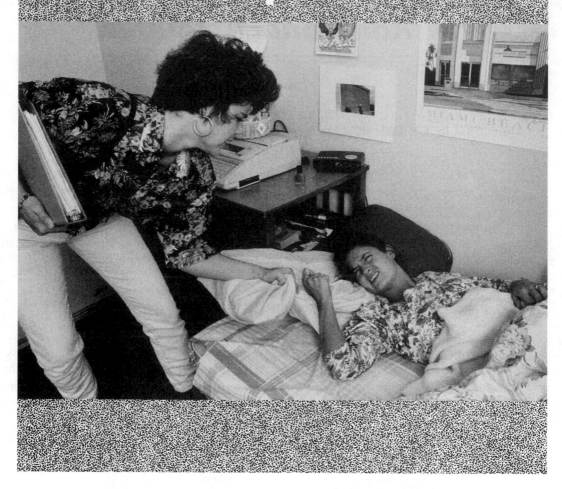

Chapter 3

Proverbs

Warm-up

THINK ABOUT THIS

Proverbs are old sayings, one or two lines long, that teach about life. Many cultures and languages have proverbs about getting up early. The following proverbs teach about the importance of early rising:

- The early bird catches the worm. (English)
- Spring is the best time of year. Morning is the best time of day. (Chinese)
- A morning riser has gold in his mouth. (Norwegian)
- Early to bed, early to rise, makes a man healthy, wealthy, and wise. (American)

In your native language, are there any proverbs about getting up early?

☰ With a Partner

1. Talk over any of the proverbs above that you do not understand.
2. Decide which one you like best and make a drawing of it together.
3. Share any other proverbs about early rising that you know. Write them on the board. Your classmates will do the same. Discuss them.

JOURNAL

Think about the proverbs told to you as a child by older family members. Choose one and write about it: Who told it to you? What was the person who said it trying to teach you? In what situation was it used? Do you think it makes sense to continue using the proverb or have times changed?

Preparation

TEN COMMON PROVERBS IN ENGLISH

The following are ten common proverbs in English. Each proverb teaches a little lesson: a cultural value that is or was important to Americans. The historical origin, or where each proverb came from, is also listed.

Proverb	Value	Origin
1. Blood is thicker than water.	Family	Scotland
2. Too many cooks spoil the broth.	Loyalty	England
	Individualism	
3. The squeaky wheel gets the oil.	Assertiveness	Unknown
4. God helps those who help themselves.	Self-help	Greece (Aeschylus)
5. Haste makes waste.	Patience	England
6. Time is money.	Efficiency	U.S. (Ben Franklin)
7. What goes around comes around.	Morality	African-American
8. Don't count your chickens before they hatch.	Caution	Greece (Aeschylus)
9. Eye for an eye, tooth for a tooth	Justice	Bible
10. Never put off 'til tomorrow what you can do today.	Efficiency	U.S.

≡ Pair Work

1. Do you understand the literal meaning of each proverb above, that is, what the words say? Paraphrase each one: Write a sentence with the same meaning, using your own words. Discuss the proverbs and then take turns writing sentences on one piece of paper.

2. Do you understand the real meaning of each, the lesson or value that each proverb expresses? Look at the photographs on page 61 and decide which proverb from the list above fits each one best. Under each photograph, write the proverb that you might use in that situation. Take turns writing with your partner.

3. Think of other situations in which you might use the proverbs in the list above. Choose one and act it out or draw it with your partner. Then share what you do with another pair.

☰ With a Partner from the Same Language Background

1. Are there any proverbs in your native language that express the same values as the ten American proverbs listed? First, list the proverbs that translate exactly into the proverbs listed on page 60. Then, list the proverbs that mean the same thing, or teach the same value, using different examples. Translate these into English.
2. Can you see examples of the values listed on page 60 in American culture or in how Americans act? For example, the value of *efficiency* (see proverb #6) can be seen in the popularity of American fast-food restaurants and in the way Americans buy kitchen appliances that promise to save time. Choose three of the values listed on page 60 that are typically American and give examples of how each can be seen in American daily life.

BACKGROUND READING

Proverbs, sometimes called sayings, are examples of folk wisdom. They are little lessons that older people of every culture pass down to younger people to teach them about life. Many proverbs remind people of cultural values, as the ten American proverbs on page 60 show. Values tell people how they should act and what their culture thinks is important. They teach what is right and wrong, according to a culture's way of thinking.

Since many proverbs are very old, some of the values they teach may not be as important in a culture as they once were. For example, Americans today do not pay much attention to the proverb "Haste makes waste," because in today's society getting a lot done is often more important than taking time to do everything carefully. But an understanding of past values can help in understanding present society. And many of the older values are still strong today. Benjamin Franklin, a famous American diplomat, writer, and scientist, died in 1790, but his proverb "Time is money" is taken more seriously by Americans today than ever before.

A study of proverbs from around the world shows that many of the values are the same. In many cases, though, the same idea is said in different ways. For example, a Spanish proverb translates into English as, "He who does not cry does not get fed," while in English there is a saying, "The squeaky wheel gets the oil." The lesson of both is similar — that you must let people know what you want — which is the value of assertiveness. This lesson is taught by two different examples. Similarly, courage is the value expressed by these two sayings: "The path is not hard to follow because of the rivers and the mountains, but because men are reluctant to face the mountains and the rivers" (Vietnamese) and "There is nothing to fear but fear itself" (English). Another value common in the proverbs of many cultures, especially traditional ones, is caution. The following proverbs teach people from seven different language groups the importance of being careful before acting or speaking: "Turn the tongue seven times, then speak" (French); "Have an umbrella before getting wet" (Japanese); "Before you drink the soup, blow on it" (Arabic); "First weigh [the consequences], then dare" (German); "If you don't know the ford, don't cross the stream" (Russian); "Be careful bending your head — you may break it" (Italian); "Look before you leap" (English).

While proverbs are common all over the world, there are different customs for their use. For example, though proverbs are part of the oral culture in the United States, good writers do not use them much. Famous Chinese essays, on the other hand, often begin with a Chinese proverb. Quoting a proverb shows knowledge of the past, an important Chinese value. But Americans do not value the past as much as the Chinese do. They think it is more important to think of something original, or at least to express it in a new way. Although essays should avoid using common American proverbs, it is perfectly fine to quote translations of proverbs from other languages.

Because the values of each culture are different, understanding the values of another culture can help explain how the people from that culture think and act. Understanding the values that your own culture teaches is important too. If you can accept that people from other cultures act according to their values, which are not always the values of your culture, getting along with them will be much easier. Finally, it is also important to think about your own personal values. It is possible to be proud of your culture without accepting every cultural value as your own.

GLOSSARY FOR CASE STUDY AND BACKGROUND READING
Value — what is most important to people
Spoil — ruin, damage, make something no good
Broth — clear soup
Squeaky — noisy, high-pitched
Haste — the act of hurrying, rushing, going too fast

Waste — garbage
Hatch — to come out of the egg
Loyalty — friendship; sticking by someone; fidelity
Individualism — the importance of each separate person
Assertiveness — standing up for oneself, defending oneself
Self-help — not asking for help from others, helping oneself
Patience — not hurrying or rushing, giving things time
Efficiency — getting things done on time and well
Morality — how one's actions affect others; knowing right from wrong
Revenge — punishing or hurting someone who has hurt you
Folk — popular; of the people
Wisdom — knowledge that comes from experience; understanding
Courage — bravery
Reluctant — not eager, not happy to do something
Caution — carefulness, thinking hard about something before doing it
Consequences — the results of an action, what happens because of something
Ford — a shallow place in a stream
Leap — jump
Oral — spoken
Quoting — copying, using quotation marks (") and identifying the origin

☰ With a Partner

1. Study the values listed in **boldface** above. Talk over any that you do not understand.
2. People often act in certain ways because of their values. The following situations reflect the values in the list above. Together, think about which of these values guide the actions of the people in each situation. Write down on a seperate sheet the value (or values) that you both think fits best.

   Example: Sandra waited for five years for her boyfriend to get out of jail; in all that time, she did not go out with another man. *Loyalty, patience.*

   a. Maria waited until her new grandchild was born to buy clothes.
   b. Vu teaches his children to fight back if other children hit them.
   c. After Lien's husband left her, she went out and worked two jobs to support her children.
   d. Enrique's boss told the workers to stop talking so much and work harder.
   e. Kazuko sent her American roommate the money for the telephone bill after she returned to Japan.
   f. Mrs. Jones asked each of her fourth grade students to write their own opinion of the story that the class read.
   g. Nina smelled smoke, called the fire department, and then made sure that all the other people in her building had left.

3. Write three more situations that show one or more of the values in boldface. Show them to another pair and see if they can guess the values.

A 4-leaf clover, walking under a ladder, the number 13, a black cat, a rabbit's foot

THINK ABOUT THIS

Proverbs are just one example of folk wisdom, or traditional beliefs. Superstition, the belief in good and bad luck, is another example of folk wisdom. The objects pictured above represent common American superstitions.

Can you tell which objects are believed to bring good luck and which are thought to bring bad luck, according to American superstitions? Ask your teacher if you guessed correctly.

≡ With a Partner from the Same Native Country or Language Background

1. Make a list of five superstitions from your native culture. Superstitions are traditional beliefs that have not been scientifically proven. Talk over which ones might be true. Put a star by the one that is believed by more people.
2. On the board, write the superstition beside which you and your partner put a star. Place the name of the country or culture in parentheses after it. Your classmates will do the same.

≡ Take a Stand

Someone will read the list of superstitions on the blackboard. After each superstition is read, stand up if you think it might be true. Then sit down. Listen to the next one and do the same.

Interviews and Analysis

 INTERVIEW TIP: TAKING NOTES DURING AN INTERVIEW

It is important to take notes during your interview with an American informant, since you will later be analyzing and discussing in class what your informant said. Also, it is too difficult to remember answers to 12 or 13 questions. However, taking notes while asking questions and trying to follow your informant's answers is difficult, especially since English is not your native language. Here are a few tips to make it easier:

- Do not try to write down everything your informant says. That would be impossible to do and would slow things down too much.
- Instead, write down key words, phrases, and examples. For example, your informant says, "My grandparents on one side came to America from Italy when they were in their teens. On the other side, my mother's grandmother came from Ireland, and my mother's father's family goes way back. I don't even know where they were from originally. I suppose they were English." You might write down these notes: Italy — grandpts. Other side Ireland + England (?).
- Use abbreviations, like "grandpts." for *grandparents*. Some common abbreviations in English are these: + or & (and); w/ (with); = (is the same as); c. (about the time of). People usually make up their own abbreviations when taking notes too. For example, if the topic of the interview is proverbs, you might use *P.*, or if the person is talking about his or her mother quite a bit, you might write *M*. However, it is important to make sure you do not forget what your own abbreviations stand for.
- Use your native language as much as you want. Remember, the notes are for you. Also, you can probably write faster in your native language, unless translating takes too much time or is confusing for you.
- Take notes even if you use a tape recorder. Your notes do not have to be as complete if you have a tape recorder as backup, but you should take notes anyway in case it is too hard for you to understand your tape for any reason. Taking notes helps you to understand the interview better because it forces you to summarize the most important information.
- Explain to your informant why you are taking notes: because this is important information that you want to be able to go over later. This will also help you to gain more time if you need to write something down after your informant has finished speaking. For example, you can say: "That's interesting. Hold on a minute while I get that down."
- Even though your head will be down while you are taking notes, try to provide nonverbal feedback to your informant anyway. Shake your head up and down, commenting "Oh, I see," or raise your eyes often to look at your informant while he or she is answering a question.

- Make sure you understand and can pronounce all of the interview questions. Review them just before the interview.
- At times, it is important to copy down exactly what the informant says, word for word. For example, in the interview about proverbs, you need to get the exact proverb written down. To make sure you get it exactly right, you can ask, "Would you mind writing that out for me?" Or ask your informant to spell certain words or repeat the proverb.

≡ Practice

1. Write down five abbreviations that you usually use or plan to start using. Look at the examples on page 65.
2. Interview a partner for three minutes about his or her plans for the weekend. Practice taking notes by writing down key words and using abbreviations. Do not forget to give nonverbal feedback while writing (see page 65). At the end of three minutes, use your notes to give your partner a summary of what was said. Share your notes with your partner and get feedback about whether your note-taking got in the way of doing a good interview. Then switch roles and let your partner practice taking notes while interviewing you.

Questionnaire 1

TRADITIONAL PROVERBS FROM YOUR CULTURE

Directions: *Older people usually know more proverbs. If possible, interview an older person from your native culture to find out about five traditional proverbs. Give a few examples of proverbs first (perhaps the one you wrote about in your journal). If you cannot find an older person from your culture to interview, think of five proverbs or sayings that you heard as a child. Or work with another student who speaks your native language. First, write down each proverb in your native language. Then translate it into English and ask your informant the following questions about each — or answer them yourself.*

Proverb #1: (in original language)

1. In English:
2. Explain what it means:
3. Describe a situation in which it would be used:
4. What is the value or lesson taught?
5. Is it used much today?
6. Do you know the origin (where it comes from)?

Proverb #2:

1. In English:
2. Meaning:
3. Situation:
4. Value:
5. Used today?
6. Origin:

Proverb #3:

1. In English:
2. Meaning:
3. Situation:
4. Value:
5. Used today?
6. Origin:

Proverb #4:

1. In English:
2. Meaning:
3. Situation:
4. Value:
5. Used today?
6. Origin:

Proverb #5:

1. In English:
2. Meaning:
3. Situation:
4. Value:
5. Used today?
6. Origin:

Signature of your informant or partner: _____ Sex: ____

Age: _____ Place of birth: _____

WITH A PARTNER FROM A DIFFERENT LANGUAGE BACKGROUND

1. Share your proverbs with each other, explaining the meanings.
2. Which one was your favorite? Explain why.
3. Make a list of any proverbs that are similar in both languages.

ALL-AMERICAN VALUES

competition   individualism
materialism   change
practicality   efficiency
informality   action
equality   self-help
honesty

....
THINK ABOUT THIS

On page 67 is a list of the most common values in the dominant American culture today, according to experts.

Which of these values is very important to you?

☰ With a Partner from Your Cultural Background

1. Make a list of the values that you think are important to most people in your native culture.
2. Talk over which of these values is also important to each of you.

Questionnaire 2: Out-of-class

TRADITIONAL AMERICAN PROVERBS

Directions: *Interview an American to learn five more proverbs. Use the following question-naire. Since older people often know more proverbs, you might have better success if you interview someone older. Or you can interview several people: Ask one person for two proverbs and ask someone else for three. At the end of the interview, write down any new vocabulary that you learned.*

Proverb #1:
Can you tell me a proverb in English, such as "The early bird catches the worm"?

_____

_____

   1. Could you explain what it really means, what the message is?

     _____

     _____

   2. What situation would it be used in?

     _____

     _____

3. What value would you say it teaches (for example: patience, caution, family)?

_____

4. Do you think the values expressed in this proverb are still important in American society today?

_____

5. Is the proverb used much today?

_____

6. Do you know the origin of the proverb (the Bible, for example)?

_____

7. Do you associate this proverb with a particular person or situation?

_____

Proverb #2:
What is another American proverb?

_____

_____

_____

1. Could you explain what it really means, what the message is?

_____

_____

2. What situation would it be used in?

_____

_____

3. What value would you say it teaches (for example: patience, caution, family)?

_____

4. Do you think the values expressed in this proverb are still important in American society today?

_____

5. Is the proverb used much today?

_____

6. Do you know the origin of the proverb (the Bible, for example)?

_____

7. Do you associate this proverb with a particular person or situation?

_____

Proverb #3:
Do you know another traditional American proverb?

_____

_____

1. Meaning:

_____

_____

2. Situation:

_____

_____

3. Value:

_____

4. Values still important?

_____

5. Proverb used today?

_____

6. Origin:

_____

7. Person/situation associated with proverb:

_____

Proverb #4:
Do you know any proverbs that are from your own ethnic background? For example, sayings that your grandparents used? (If not, ask about another traditional American proverb.)

_____

_____

_____

_____

1. Meaning:

_____

_____

2. Situation:

_____

_____

3. Value:

_____

4. Values still important?

_____

5. Proverb used today?

_____

6. Origin:

_____

7. Person/situation associated with proverb:

_____

Proverb #5:
Do you know any other proverbs that were traditional in your family? (Or find out another American proverb.)

_____

_____

_____

_____

1. Meaning:

_____

_____

2. Situation:

_____

_____

3. Value:

_____

4. Values still important?

_____

5. Proverb used today?

_____

6. Origin:

_____

7. Person/situation associated with proverb:

_____

American informant interviewed: _____ Sex: ____

Ethnic background: _____ Place of birth: _____

New vocabulary: _____

ANALYSIS ON YOUR OWN

1. Look over the five proverbs in English that you wrote on Questionnaire 2. Are there any proverbs in your native language that mean something similar, or that people would use in the same kind of situation? (If there are, write them in your native language, then translate into English, next to the similar English proverb.)
2. Look over the values that your American informant said were communicated by the American proverbs. Write down those that are also important to you personally.
3. Look over the values that were expressed by the proverbs in your native language (see Questionnaire 1). Write the one that you think is the most important in your culture today:
4. Do any of the traditional proverbs from your culture that you wrote down seem old-fashioned, that is, more about the past than about your native culture today? Write down the proverbs (translated into English) that do not seem to apply as much to your native culture today.

ANALYSIS IN A SMALL GROUP

Work in groups of three. Choose a **reporter** for the group (to tell the whole class about your discussion), a **checker** (to make sure everyone can answer question 6 below), and a **leader**, (to ask the group to talk over the following questions).

1. How did your interview with an American go? Talk over any problems.
2. How did you do at taking notes and interviewing at the same time? Talk over any problems. Decide on some suggestions for taking notes during interviews. Write down a list of abbreviations that each person used while taking notes.
3. What were some of the differences between interviewing someone from your own background, in your native language, and interviewing an American?
4. Was there an American proverb that you did not understand? (The checker will write these down and bring them to the class discussion.)
5. What was your favorite American proverb?
6. As a group, choose one of these American proverbs that everybody likes. Learn it by heart. Then plan a skit, a short drama, or a play that shows the truth of the proverb your group chose. Practice acting it out. Write the proverb out in large letters on a piece of paper.

ANALYSIS IN CLASS

1. Proverbs quiz:
   - First, each group will write their chosen proverb in large letters and give the paper to the teacher.
   - Next, the teacher will tape all the papers to the wall or board.
   - Present the skits planned in the small groups to the rest of the class.
   - After each skit is performed, the class will choose which proverb it is about (from the list of proverbs taped to the board).
2. Discuss the American proverbs that the groups of three did not understand. The checker from each small group will write these on the board for everyone to see.
3. The reporter from each group will write on the board the abbreviations used during interviews and share suggestions about note-taking. Discuss these.
4. Discuss these questions about American informants that were interviewed:
   - Which informants were better able to identify five proverbs: Older or younger? Males or females? People from any particular birthplace?
   - From what ethnic backgrounds did American informants come? How many of the American informants were able to remember proverbs from their ethnic backgrounds? From which backgrounds? What does this say about people keeping their cultures in the United States?
5. What American values are reflected by the English language proverbs collected by the class? List other examples of those values that can be seen in everyday life in the United States.

JOURNAL

What proverbs do you think are important for your own children to know? Select two or three and explain why these are important to you.

Additional Activities

BUMPER STICKER SURVEY*

The sayings on bumper stickers are like modern-day proverbs because many of them express the values important to the car's owner. For example, "Kiss Me: I'm Irish," a popular bumper sticker, and bumper stickers with flags communicate ethnic pride and/or patriotism. Another popular bumper sticker, "Think Globally, Act Locally," is about social activism, or community involvement. Many bumper stickers are intended to be funny, but humor is different in every culture. To learn more about American values through studying bumper stickers:

1. Find at least three bumper stickers on cars on the street. Write down what they say and bring the list to class.
2. On the board, write down your favorite bumper sticker from your list. Your classmates will do the same.
3. As a class, decide which value each American bumper sticker stands for.
4. From the list of bumper stickers on the board, rank them in order of humor (put a 1 next to the funniest).
5. Copy the list of bumper stickers from the blackboard onto paper. Ask an American to rank them in order of which are funniest. Compare the results and decide what makes Americans laugh.

* This activity was developed by Sheila Becker.

METAPHORS

I. **Metaphors in Proverbs.**
Many proverbs are metaphors. (Metaphors tell about something by describing something else that is similar in some way.) For example, "The early bird catches the worm" is a message about people, not just birds. The "worm" in this proverb is a metaphor for the good things that come to people who get up early.
   Work with a partner to identify the metaphors in the following American proverbs:

Example: Don't cry over spilt [spilled] milk. *spilt milk = what has already happened.*

1. You've made your bed, now lie in it. *bed =* _____

2. A watched pot never boils. *watched pot =* _____

3. Don't judge a book by its cover. *book =* _____

4. Write another proverb that contains a metaphor.

II. Metaphors in poetry.

Poets use metaphors to suggest new ways of looking at the world. For example, the following poem by the famous American poet Carl Sandburg is a description of fog, the water in the air that makes it difficult to see. He uses the metaphor of a cat to describe how fog moves:

Fog

The fog comes
on little cat feet.

It sits looking over harbor and city
on silent haunches
and then moves on.

Read the following poems, which are also metaphors. Then answer the questions:

Clouds
by Christina Rossetti

White sheep, white sheep
On a blue hill.
When the wind stops
You all stand still.
When the wind blows
You walk away slow.
White sheep, white sheep,
Where do you go?

1. What are sheep a metaphor for in this poem?
2. What is the hill a metaphor for?
3. What is the meaning of the last line?

The Hungry Waves
by Dorothy Aldis

The hungry waves along the shore
Chase each other with a roar.

They raise their heads and, wide and high,
Toss their hair against the sky.

They show their teeth in rows of white
And open up their jaws to bite.

4. In the central metaphor of this poem, what are waves being compared to? Hair? White teeth?

5. In your opinion, which poem has the best metaphor? Explain why you like it.

III. Metaphors in Everyday Language.

People use metaphors in their everyday speech, often without realizing it. Metaphors make our language more colorful and rich. Some examples of metaphors from colloquial American speech are listed in the column on the left. Draw a line to match the metaphors below to their correct definition.

He's a real *pain in the neck.*	Exhausted; overworked
The exam was *a piece of cake.*	In a difficult position
His idea is *pie in the sky.*	Easy
The movie was *dynamite.*	Unable to concentrate; daydreaming
The choice put me *between a rock and a hard place.*	Powerful; great
His story sounded *fishy.*	Very busy
I've been *in a fog* all day.	Not quite right; suspicious; rotten
Don't *rock the boat/Don't make waves.*	A bother
I've been *tied up* all day.	Impossible
He is *burned out* from his job.	Make trouble; call attention to

≡ With a Partner from the Same Language Background

1. List five metaphors that are used as idioms in your language. Translate them into English and write them in sentences.

2. Share these metaphors with another pair of classmates from a different language background.

3. Tell your partner to close the book and tell you the definitions of half of the idioms in italics above. Then close your book and give the definitions of the other half of the idioms above while your partner quizzes you.

Chapter 4

Manners

Warm-up

As you were growing up, what did your parents try to teach you about "table manners," how to act during a meal? Do you think these "rules" are the same around the world?

1. Make a list of five **do's**: the five things your parents told you were most important to do at mealtimes.
2. Make a list of the five most important mealtime **don'ts**: what you were told never to do.

≡ With a Partner

1. Compare your lists of do's and don'ts.
2. Make a new list of any items that both of you wrote that were the same.

≡ With Another Pair

1. Compare your latest lists of do's and don'ts that were the same.
2. Make a new list of only those items that were the same for all four.
3. Write the new list on the board. Other groups of four will do the same.
4. Make a new list of do's and don'ts that were listed by everyone in the class. Find out from your teacher if the items on the list are taught in American families too.

JOURNAL

When you are invited to someone's home for dinner or for a party, what are some of the things you try to remember to do so that your host will think you are a polite guest? Write about how you try to act when you visit someone at their home.

Preparation

CASE STUDY

John, an American, was very glad to be invited to a dinner party to celebrate the graduation of his neighbor, Mazen, who was from Saudi Arabia. John had never been to a Saudi party before, and he did not know what to bring. He finally decided on a bottle of good champagne, which he tied with a bright red ribbon.

When John got to the party, he could tell that Mazen was glad to see him. Mazen put his arm around John's shoulder, saying, "Oh, John. I'm so glad you could come."

John answered, "I wouldn't have missed it." He handed Mazen the bottle of champagne as he said, "Congratulations."

Mazen took the champagne. Then he said, "Come meet my sister. She arrived from Ryad just two days ago."

Mazen's arm was still on John's shoulder. Trying to be just as friendly and warm as his host, John reached out and put his arm around Mazen's sister, saying: "Hey, any sister of Mazen's is a friend of mine."

Mazen stopped smiling. He took John's elbow, moving him across the room to a table of drinks. "What can I get you to drink, John?" he asked.

John enjoyed himself very much at the party that night. He couldn't believe how much food had been prepared — far more than the guests could possibly eat. He decided that Mazen must have invited many more people than had actually come. As John was leaving, he realized that Mazen had not opened the champagne, or even thanked him for it. He decided that because of all the excitement, Mazen had probably forgotten all about it.

☰ On Your Own

Write down the answers to these questions. Skip a line after each answer.

1. What were some of the ways that John tried to be a polite guest?
2. What were some of the ways that Mazen tried to be a polite host?
3. Why didn't Mazen open the champagne?
4. Explain what happened when John put his arm around Mazen's sister.
5. Why did Mazen serve so much food?

≡ With Two Other Classmates

1. Take turns reading the answers you wrote.
2. Talk them over.
3. If you learned something new from a classmate's answers, add it to your own.

....

THINK ABOUT THIS

In the United States, most brides wear white, the traditional American color of purity. In China, where red is the color of happiness, many brides wear red.

1. In your native country, what color do brides wear and why?
2. What other colors are worn on special occasions?
3. Do colors have any other meanings when they are worn by certain people?

≡ With a Partner from Your Native Culture

1. Talk over your ideas and thoughts about the questions above.
2. Make up a list of statements about the meaning of wearing certain colors where you come from.

≡ Ask Your Teacher

Go around the class and take turns asking your teacher if the meanings given to certain colors are the same in the United States.

BACKGROUND READING

What is polite in one culture is sometimes quite *im*polite in another culture, as the chapter on body language showed. In the case study, John tried hard to be a polite guest according to the customs of his culture. That is why he brought champagne as a gift, for Americans drink champagne to celebrate important occasions such as weddings. It is also common — though not necessary — for Americans to bring food or a bottle of wine to an informal party. When invited to someone's house for a meal, many will ask, "What can I bring?" In fact, at some American parties the guests bring almost all the food; these are called *potlucks*. The potluck is an example of the American values of informality and fairness: At a potluck, everyone shares the costs and work of preparing for the party.

A similar American custom is "B.Y.O.B.," which appears on many party invitations in the United States. These letters stand for "bring your own bottle" or "bring you own booze" (a slang expression for liquor). It is not *always* a good idea to bring liquor to a party in the United States, though. Most states do not allow anyone under the ages of 18 or 21 to buy liquor, and in some families, and in some religions, people do not drink alcohol. Social customs or rules about alcohol are changing for many Americans. For example, people today think more about the fact that driving after drinking alcohol is not safe. For this reason, friends who go out together often ask one person not to drink so that he or she can be the "designated driver" for the group.

Though by American standards John's champagne was a lovely gift, by Saudi standards it was most *im*polite. The main reason is that alcohol is against the Muslim religion. It seems that Mazen was too polite to say so. Another reason is that hospitality, showing what a generous host you are, is a very important value in Arab cultures. That is why Mazen's party had more food than the guests could eat, for example. In many cultures where generosity is valued, a guest can insult his or her host by bringing along food or drink. The host might think the guest is afraid that there will not be enough to eat or drink at the party.

John also showed little understanding of Arab culture when he put his arm around Mazen's sister. From his point of view, he was trying to be polite by copying his host's friendly gesture. But in Muslim cultures, the most *im*polite thing a man can do is to touch a woman who is not his wife. John put his arm around Mazen's sister to show his friendship with Mazen. But to an Arab, that gesture shows the opposite: that John does not respect his sister. For that reason, it is an insult to Mazen as well.

People all over the world want respect from others. But cultures show respect in different ways, as John's experiences at Mazen's party show. To understand these differences, it is often helpful to understand the values important to each culture, including one's own. For example, if John had understood how much Arabs value hospitality, he would not have been so surprised at all the food at Mazen's party. If he had understood the value that Saudis place on the teachings of the Muslim religion, he certainly would not have brought champagne to Mazen's party. Similarly, if others understood how much Americans value informality, directness, and fairness, they would not be surprised when they are invited to "B.Y.O.B." to American parties.

GLOSSARY FOR CASE STUDY AND BACKGROUND READING

Alcohol — beer, wine, or other kinds of liquor
Guest — someone visiting another person's home
Insult — to show disrespect; to offend; to make someone feel bad
Host — the person who invites people to his or her home
Impolite — not polite; rude; not nice
Slang — Informal language used among friends
Champagne — expensive, bubbly wine, originally from France
Standards — rules; customs; expectations
Generosity — the sharing or giving freely of whatever one has
Hospitality — making guests feel welcome; being a generous host
Table Manners — how to act when eating
Toast — the custom of saying something before drinking alcohol together
Humility — holding back or hiding one's own needs and wants
Equality — fairness; equal chance
Appropriate — right for the place and time
Potluck — a kind of party where everyone brings something

≡ With a Partner

1. Together, fill out the chart below about the Background Reading.

I. Main idea of background reading: _____

_____

A. Example given to support main idea: _____

_____

B. Example: _____

_____

C. Example: _____

_____

D. Write an example that you would include if you were the author: _____

_____

With your partner take turns reading each of the following sentences out loud. Instead of saying the word that is underlined, use a synonym or expression that means the same thing.

Example: In the Middle East, when mothers teach their children *table manners,* the first thing they tell them is never to eat with their left hand.

In the Middle East, when mothers teach their children *how to act at mealtimes,* the first thing they tell them is never to eat with their left hand.

1. Wine is part of the religious ceremony in both the Catholic and Jewish religions; however, the Muslim, Mormon, and Seventh Day Adventist religions do not allow members to drink *alcohol* of any kind.
2. John was one of the many *guests* at Mazen's party.
3. When John got to the party, his *host,* Mazen, greeted him at the door in a very friendly way.
4. In the United States, it is usually all right to politely ask your hostess for a second helping of food, though in many other cultures asking for more is *impolite.*
5. *Champagne* is a fancy kind of "booze," made from a special kind of grape.
6. The *standards* for being a good host are different from country to country; however, a good host in any culture always thinks of the comfort of the guest first.
7. In cultures where *generosity* is an important value, one never eats in front of others without first offering them some food.
8. "My house is your house" is a Spanish proverb, or saying, showing the value of *hospitality* in countries in which Spanish is spoken.
9. One way for a guest to thank his host for his hospitality is to raise his glass and say an appropriate *toast* before the meal.
10. In cultures that value *humility,* it is the custom to say no several times to offers of food before saying yes.
11. In the past 20 years, more American men have started cooking for their friends; ideas of sexual *equality* have thus given some men a new hobby.
12. Ideas of sexual equality also mean that it is now *appropriate* for male guests to help clear the dishes after a dinner party in an American home.
13. The custom of and even the word *potluck* come from a Native American celebration in which all the food in the village was shared among all.

THINK ABOUT THIS

In Japan, chrysanthemums make people think about death, while in the United States they remind people of autumn.

In your native culture, are there any flowers that have a special meaning?

≡ With a Partner

1. Talk about flowers as gifts where you each come from.
2. Share any special meanings that different flowers have in your native cultures.
3. Draw one or two of the flowers mentioned above. Decide who will draw and who will explain to the class about each flower.

≡ In Front of the Class

1. Stand up and share the drawing that your partner made with the class, explaining about the special meaning it has.
2. Listen to your classmates share their pictures and explanations.

Interviews and Analysis

INTERVIEW TIP: HELP YOUR INFORMANT TO RELAX WITH WARM-UP QUESTIONS

Though you may still be a little nervous about doing an interview, it is possible that the Americans you interview may be nervous too. One way that good interviewers help their informants to relax is by asking a few friendly questions before getting into the interview. You might ask about someone you both know, as in, "Have you seen _____ lately? How's she/he doing?" If the person is about your age, you might say something like, "So how are you doing?" (If they are older, asking, "How are you?" is a little more formal and polite.) Depending on the person, other "safe" things that you could chat about before beginning the interview are the weather or sports. Also, you could say something nice or ask a question about something special that the person is wearing.

   Developing friendly trust when people are a little nervous is known as "breaking the ice." This is especially important if you and your informant do not know each other. If this is the case, you could ask a few general questions, such as "How long have you lived here?" "Are you a student or do you work?" Don't forget nonverbal communication when trying to break the ice with your informant: Smile, look friendly, nod, and say "uh huh" when your informant answers your questions, and look him or her in the eye.

   It is also important to be careful about your informant's time. Most Americans feel like they never have enough time. So some informants who are in a hurry may want you to start the interview right away, to "get down to business."

   Practice: Choose as an interview partner someone in class whom you don't know very well.

1. Before you interview your partner, ask two or three warm-up questions.
2. Interview your partner about this: You have just heard that your best friend's grand-mother has died. What is the polite thing to do? Explain.
3. Your partner will ask you a couple of warm-up questions and then interview you about the same topic.
4. Talk about whether the warm-up questions worked to break the ice. Discuss the non-verbal communication that each interviewer used.
5. Talk over your individual plans for interviewing an American informant. Make a list of two warm-up questions that each of you will ask. Work on the extra question together too (question 15, Questionnaire 2).

Questionnaire 1: In-class

GOOD MANNERS IN _____
(your partner's native country)

Sit down with your interview partner (see above). Ask a new warm-up question. Then ask your interview partner to answer the following questions according to the customs of his or her native culture. After considering each question, circle "yes" or "no" in the column to the left of the question. Note any explanation in the space provided. Then answer the questions while your partner interviews you.

Yes No 1. Imagine that you are invited to a small dinner to celebrate the graduation of a good friend (from your culture). Do you bring along something to eat or drink? Explain.

Yes No 2. You bring your friend a gift for his graduation. Will he open it during the party? Explain.

Yes No 3. At the party, your friend introduces you to his cousin, a woman doctor who is about 30 years old. Do you call her by her first name? Explain.

Yes No 4. Your friend's cousin invites you to a party at her house next week, but you know that you will be busy then. Do you tell her you will come anyway, just to be polite? Explain.

Yes No 5. Do you ask your host for a drink if you are thirsty? Explain.

Yes No 6. Do you light up a cigarette if you feel like smoking? Explain.

Yes No 7. Your friend has a very nice house. Do you ask him how much it cost? Explain.

Yes No 8. Dinner is served and everyone sits down. Do you begin to eat? Explain.

Yes No 9. The food is delicious, but you are not really hungry. Do you eat anyway, to be polite?

Yes No 10. One of the dishes is wonderful, and you would like to try a little more. Do you ask for it?

Yes No 11. If your host asks you if you want more to eat, do you first say no, to be polite? Explain.

Yes No 12. After dinner, do you help your host take the dishes out to the kitchen, to be polite? Explain.

Yes No 13. After eating, everyone leaves the table to relax. Are you shocked when your host sits down and puts his feet up on a nearby chair? Explain.

Yes No 14. Several days after the party, you want to tell your friend what a good time you had. Would you stop by his house without calling first? Explain.

Signature of interview partner: _____

Place of birth: _____ Time in U.S.: _____

THINK ABOUT THIS

The most common American toasts are "Cheers" or "Here's to _____" (a person's name, health, etc.). Two other American toasts may sound funny the first time you hear them: "Bottoms up" and "Here's mud in your eye." Though Americans are not known for their poetic toasts, they often enjoy toasts from other lands and languages. When eating or drinking with Americans, it is nice to be able to offer a toast translated into English from your language.

1. Are there any common toasts in your native language?
2. Write them down in your native language.

☰ With a Partner Who Speaks Your Native Language

1. Compare the toasts that you wrote down.
2. Select one that you both like and translate it into English. Practice saying it.

☰ Toasting in Circles: (Bring a drink to class to make this more fun!)

1. Stand up with your classmates and go to a part of the room that is large enough to hold everyone.
2. Decide with your partner which one of you will be on the *outside circle* and which one will be on the *inside circle.*
3. Make a circle of all the students who decided to be on the inside circle. Holding hands, face out. Around the inside circle, form an outside circle of the rest of the students, who will hold hands and face *in.* Students in both circles will face each other and drop hands.
4. Facing the classmate across from you, raise your hand as if you had a glass in it, and say the toast from your culture, first in your native language and then in English. Ask the classmate to raise his or her imaginary glass and repeat your toast after you in English. Then toast each other again, repeating the toast from your classmate's native language translated into English.
5. While the outside circle stands still, those of you in the inside circle will move a few steps to the left until you are facing a different classmate from the one you just toasted. After rotating once like this so that you have a new toasting partner, toast each other like you just did. Repeat, rotating the inner circle, until you have toasted all your classmates in the other circle.

Questionnaire 2: Out-of-class

GOOD MANNERS IN THE U.S.

Interview an American with the following questionnaire. Don't forget to ask your warm-up questions before the interview starts. When you begin your interview with the following questionnaire, ask the person to try to answer the questions with a yes or no, and then to explain. Make up one question of your own. Write down any new vocabulary at the bottom of the questionnaire.

Yes   No   1. Imagine that you are invited to a small dinner to celebrate the graduation of a friend. Do you bring along something to eat or drink? Explain.

_____

_____

Yes No   2. You bring your friend a gift for his graduation. Will he open it during the party? Explain.

_____

Yes No   3. At the party, your friend introduces you to his female cousin, a doctor who is about 30 years old. Do you call her by her first name? Explain.

_____

Yes No   4. Your friend's cousin invites you to a party at her house next week, but you know that you will be busy then. Do you tell her you will come anyway, just to be polite? Explain.

_____

Yes No   5. Do you ask your host for a drink if you are thirsty? Explain.

_____

Yes No   6. Do you light up a cigarette if you feel like smoking? Explain.

_____

Yes No   7. Your friend has a very nice house. Do you ask him how much it cost? Explain.

_____

Yes No   8. Dinner is served and everyone sits down. Do you begin to eat? Explain.

_____

Yes No   9. The food is delicious, but you are not really hungry. Do you eat anyway, to be polite?

_____

Yes No 10. One of the dishes is wonderful, and you would like to try a little more. Do you ask for it?

_____

Yes No 11. If your host asks you if you want more to eat, do you first say no to be polite? Explain.

_____

Yes No 12. After dinner, do you help your host take the dishes out to the kitchen, to be polite? Explain.

_____

Yes No 13. After eating, everyone leaves the table to relax. Are you shocked when your host sits down and puts his feet up on a nearby chair? Explain.

_____

Yes No 14. Several days after the party, you want to tell your friend what a good time you had. Would you stop by his house without calling first? Explain.

_____

Yes No 15. Your own question.

_____

Signature of American interviewed: _____ Sex: _____

Place of birth: _____

Race, religion, or ethnic background: _____

New vocabulary: _____

ANALYSIS ON YOUR OWN

Compare the yes/no answers that you wrote down on both Questionnaires.

1. How many of the same questions received the same response (*yes* or *no*) on both questionnaires? _____
2. In the space below, write the number of each question that received *different* responses, that is, "yes" on one questionnaire and "no" on another. _____
3. Look over Questionnaire 2 and choose any answer that you did not understand completely. Write down your question to share with your small group.

ANALYSIS IN A SMALL GROUP

Bring the notes from your Questionnaires and your Individual Analysis to discuss with two classmates. Choose as the **secretary** someone who has not done this job before. The secretary will fill out the chart below, but he or she does not have to write the answers to any other questions. Then choose a **discussion leader** to ask the group the following questions and to make sure that everyone gets a chance to talk. Pick a **timekeeper** to make sure that the group finishes on time. Take turns answering these questions:

1. Who did you interview and why?
2. Share the warm-up questions that you each asked and talk about whether asking them helped to make things friendlier. How comfortable did your American informant seem during the interview?
3. Choose one word to describe your interview. Explain.
4. Tell about any problems that you had doing the interview. Ask the others in the group what they would have done. If you cannot think of a solution, and you feel it might be a problem in the next interview as well, discuss it with the teacher.
5. Talk about an answer to Questionnaire 2 that you did not understand.
6. Share the information you learned from asking your own question (#15).
7. Together, fill out the chart below to find out if all of your American informants answered the questions in the same way. The secretary will record your answers.

AMERICAN ANSWERS TO QUESTIONNAIRE 2

Questions	YES	NO	Questions	YES	NO
1			8		
2			9		
3			10		
4			11		
5			12		
6			13		
7			14		

If there were any questions that were answered differently by the Americans your group interviewed, discuss how the Americans explained their answers. Do you think that their age, sex, or background are the reason for the difference in customs?

8. What American values are shown in the answers given by your American informants? (For example: fairness, equality, informality.)

ANALYSIS IN CLASS

1. The secretary from each group will write on the board one warm-up question that worked for someone in the group. Talk about those questions.

2. A bar graph on the board will summarize the information that each group filled out on their chart (Small-Group Analysis Question 7). The secretary from each group will fill in the number of boxes on the graph that show the number of "yes" and "no" answers the members of the group received on each question. Complete and copy this graph on the board to show how the Americans answered each question.

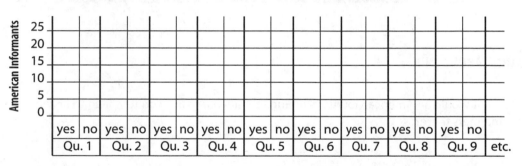

3. After looking over the finished bar graph, talk about what it means: How much do Americans agree on social customs? What are some of the different customs that account for the questions with similar numbers of "yes" and "no" responses on the bar graph? Can these differences be explained by differences in age, background, sex, etc.?

4. Each discussion leader will write on the board one American value that his or her small group thought was shown by an answer to Questionnaire 2. In what other ways do these American values appear in daily life in the United States?

JOURNAL

Write about your discussion in a small group of three. What did you learn from your classmates? How well did your group work as a group? Write about some of the positive and negative things about working in the group. OR: Write about a time when you felt confused or embarrassed in a social situation in the United States. Tell about the situation, how you felt, and what you did. Then write about how you understand it now, and what you would do if you were in the same situation today.

THINK ABOUT THIS

What would an American tourist planning to visit your native country need to know about manners there?

≡ **With a Partner from Your Native Country**

1. Together, make up a list of do's and don'ts for a visitor who wants to fit in. You can focus on do's and don'ts at the table, in clothing, or in general social customs.
2. Brainstorm the list together. Then decide who will write the do's and who will write the don'ts.

Additional Activities

USING "EXCUSE ME," "THANKS," "PLEASE," AND "SORRY"

"Excuse me," "Thank You" (or "Thanks,") "Please," and "Sorry" are the oil that makes the American machinery of social interaction run smoothly. People from other countries are often surprised and confused at the amount of apologizing and thanking that Americans do. Yet Americans expect to hear these words frequently, on all sorts of minor social occasions.

With a partner, decide which of these three expressions should be used on the following occasions. (In some cases, one of several answers is correct, and in other cases more than one answer can be used.) Write down the expression or expressions and then act out the situation.

Example: After dinner, at a friend's house, you burp. *"Excuse me."*

1. On a public bus, you touch another passenger's arm accidentally.

   "_____"

2. A friend tells you how nice you look.

   "_____"

3. You ask the person sitting next to you to pass the sugar.

   "_____"

4. In a restaurant, you go up to two waitresses who are having a conversation to find out where the bathroom is.

   "_____"

5. The postal clerk gives you your package.

   "_____"

6. You are five minutes late for class.

   "_____"

7. In class, you ask the teacher to repeat a homework assignment.

   "_____"

8. At a dinner party, you begin to yawn.

   "_____"

9. Your teacher hands back your homework.

   "_____"

10. You are in a cafeteria line, and the woman in front of you is filling up several cups with soda, but you are ready to pay.

    "_____"

11. You pay for soda with a $20 bill, the smallest bill you have.

    "_____"

12. You call someone up on the phone after 10:00 P.M.

    "_____"

13. During a conversation with a friend, you can't stop sneezing.

    "_____"

14. By accident, you open the bathroom door when someone is inside.

    "_____"

15. You ask a stranger in the street where the bus stop is. (use two)

    "_____"

······················
ADVICE COLUMNS

Many American newspapers carry advice columns to help people figure out how to act in difficult social situations. The following letter is an example of someone asking for advice.

Dear Mr. Goodmanners:

I have a problem that I need some advice on. My roommate and I get along very well. I also like her boyfriend. But whenever he comes over, he smokes the whole time — and it really bothers me. Do you have any suggestions about how to handle this without offending anyone?

Sincerely,

Can't Breathe at Home

With a partner, write an answer to Can't Breathe. Share it with the class. Then work with your partner to think of a "problem" that someone might write to Mr. Goodmanners about. Write a short letter and make two copies. Get together with two other pairs and trade letters. Pretend that you and your partner are Mr. Goodmanners and make up answers to the two letters given to you by the other pairs. Write letters back to them. When everyone has finished, get together in your group of six and share responses.

Chapter 5

Work

Warm-up

In this family, several members are in the field of medicine. A field is a general area or kind of work, such as education or business. Think about these questions and make notes about your answers.

1. Do two or more people in your family do the same kind of work?
2. Do you know other families in which several members work in the same field? What field or fields?
3. What do you think are some reasons why family members often go into the same kind of work?

With a Partner

1. Talk over your answers to the questions above.
2. Together, make a list of four reasons why it is common for people in the same family to do similar work. Give examples.
3. Share your reasons with the class.

JOURNAL

When you were a child, what kind of job or profession did you dream of doing when you grew up? Why? Write about your career plans, beginning in childhood. Include answers to these questions: What kind of work would you like to be doing in five years? What will you need to do in order to achieve this goal? How does learning English fit in?

Preparation

Toan drove to the office building where his cousin Hien worked as a computer programmer. He found her at her computer. After they had greeted each other, she took him to the employee lounge. She said, "I told you that I had spoken to my boss about you for the part-time programming job. I'm sorry. I thought everything was all set. Now he says that you'll need to go through a couple of interviews, one with him, and one with the manager of the department. Then he'll give you a 30-day tryout. He always plays it straight."

"Oh," said Toan. "Maybe they're afraid their whole programming department will become Vietnamese."

"That wouldn't bother them. They think that we're all born with superior programming ability. I'm pretty sure you'll get the job, but the company never hires anyone without going through the interview process. Have you had many interviews?" she asked.

"This is my first. Remember, I'm still in school. What did they ask you when you interviewed for your job, Hien?"

"Let me see, weird questions like, 'Tell us about your strengths and weaknesses' and 'Are you a responsible person?' Then there was a really crazy one, 'Tell us why we should hire you.' They seem to want you to sound like either a fool or a show-off. They're certainly not looking for a polite Vietnamese answer. And make sure to tell them why you want to work for them more than any other company."

"So they want you to lie too?"

Hien laughed. "I can see you haven't been to many job interviews. Did you bring a resumé?"

"No, I don't have any work experience. But I did bring my high school diploma."

"Forget it. Do a resumé and put down that programming you did for Uncle Vu at his store. Even if you weren't paid, it will look good."

Toan looked very unsure and wondered if he was really ready to enter the world of work.

GLOSSARY FOR VOCABULARY USED IN CASE STUDY

Lounge — a room used for relaxing and sometimes eating

Tryout — a new job, with pay, given for a certain period of time until it is decided whether to hire the new worker or not

To play it straight — to follow all the rules

Weird — unusual, strange

Show-off — someone who tells others how great he or she is (also a verb, written "to show off")

Resumé — a document that shows someone's work and education history (see pp. 113-114)

THINK ABOUT THIS

1. How did Hien help her cousin?
2. Why did Toan feel he was not ready for the world of work?
3. What do you think Toan needs to do to get this job?
4. Was it a good idea for Toan to bring his diploma? Explain.
5. Do you think Hien's company was racist?
6. How do you feel about answering the questions that they asked Hien?
7. Are job interviews as common in other countries? Are they similar?
8. In your native country, is there ever job discrimination, that is, do people sometimes not get jobs because of their religion, ethnic background, class, or gender?

☰ With a Partner

1. Talk over your answers to the questions above.
2. Answer them in writing together. Take turns writing down the answer to each question.

THINK ABOUT THIS

On most jobs in the United States, employees are given short periods of time off every morning and afternoon for a "coffee break," though not everyone drinks coffee.

In your native country, what kind of breaks are employees allowed?

☰ With a Partner

1. Talk over the customs of breaks in your native countries and discuss the good and bad points of each.
2. Decide what you would do about giving employees breaks during the workday if you were the boss.

BACKGROUND READING

Toan probably had a better chance of getting the programming job because of his cousin, but the company Hien worked for was careful not to hire him just because they were cousins. This is typical of an American business. While some other cultures think it natural and positive for relatives to work together in the same organization, many American companies see it as a negative thing. Many even have rules against "nepotism," which is a negative word for people hiring relatives — especially if one is the boss — in a business that has other employees. These rules may reflect the American values of equality and fairness: People should be hired because of what they can do, not who they know. Another way to look at it is that in American business, work is often more important than people. In spite of these rules, Americans often do get jobs because of who they know. This is known as "using pull" or "having connections" in slang terms.

Although pull certainly helps, most American companies make job applicants go through a formal process of applying for a job. This process usually requires one or more interviews with the employer. The questions that Hien had to answer are typical. "Tell us your strengths" is a question that job applicants are supposed to answer by doing just that, talking about what good workers they are. The answer that American employers expect to hear, the "right" answer, requires job applicants to be assertive, which is an important value in American culture. The questions Hien was asked sounded crazy to her because the opposite value, humility, especially with superiors, is required in Vietnamese culture. Yet Hien was bicultural enough to understand the conflict in cultural values, for she advised her cousin not to give a "polite Vietnamese answer."

The job interview is a ritual in American culture. A ritual is a custom that must always be done in the same way. Though the social rituals vary from culture to culture, every culture has its own. For example, other cultures have different rituals for applying for work, and a job interview is not always included. In much of the world, a necessary part of the ritual of job application is showing one's diplomas. Because this does not happen to be part of the American job application ritual, most American employers would think it unusual or even weird if an applicant brought along his or her actual diplomas. Instead, American businesses require applicants to bring a resumé, fill out a job application, and sometimes to bring along original transcripts (not copies) of their grades. Another American employment ritual is the recommendation by a former employer or teacher, called a reference. This can be given in the form of a letter, or the job applicant may be asked to give the telephone number of a reference. In this case, it is always polite to ask someone beforehand, "Will you be a reference for me if they call you from Company X, where I'm applying for a job?"

The American employment ritual was new to Toan, and he seemed to be experiencing culture shock. It is natural to feel scared and nervous about applying for work in one's own culture, but it is especially hard when so many of the rituals are new. It is even more difficult when the rituals demand behavior that goes against one's cultural values, as Hien realized. She knew that she had to give answers that in her culture would be considered impolite and disrespectful. Culture shock can be reduced by understanding how the interview ritual is culturally programmed. It is also helpful to practice the ritual ahead of time. Many job applicants, even Americans, role-play job interviews with others to prepare themselves for the real situation.

GLOSSARY FOR BACKGROUND READING VOCABULARY

Applicant — someone who applies for something, in this case, someone looking for a job

Employment — paid work (employer = boss)

Assertive — able to stand up for oneself, not shy

Humility — respect for others; not wanting to make a show of one's own abilities or achievements; modesty

Conflict — difference; disagreement

Bicultural — able to get along in two cultures

Transcripts — the official grade report of a student

Culture shock — difficulty in getting used to cultural differences

Reduced — made less, smaller

☰ With a Partner

1. Talk over anything in the Background Reading that you did not understand.
2. Make up two good study questions about what happened in the reading. Begin one with "What" and the other with "Who."

   Example: What made Hien laugh?

3. Ask another pair to answer your questions. Then answer theirs.
4. Repeat, exchanging questions with another pair.

IN A SMALL GROUP

1. A **field** is a large area of employment that includes many *positions,* or *jobs.* Together, match up the fields on the left with the positions on the right. After each field, write the number of each position, or positions, that are part of the field. Note: Several fields should have more than one position listed after them, and several positions should be listed more than once.

FIELDS	POSITIONS
Medicine _____	1. Sales Representative
Business _____	2. Social Worker
Education _____	3. Secretary
Food Industry _____	4. Nurse
High Technology _____	5. Custodian, cleaning person
Social Services _____	6. Computer Programmer
	7. Dishwasher
	8. Technician
	9. Office Worker
	10. Accountant
	11. Director of Personnel

THINK ABOUT THIS

Every year more American workplaces ban smoking. Some employers allow employees to smoke only in certain areas.

1. What do you think of this policy?
2. Would it ever happen in your native country?

☰ With a Partner

1. Talk over your answers.
2. Make a list of all the workplaces that you know of that have banned smoking.
3. Write your list on the board.

Interviews and Analysis

 INTERVIEW TIP: VOCABULARY AND JARGON USED IN THE WORKING WORLD

Jargon is vocabulary that is used in special ways in different fields. Many fields have their own jargon, which is often not understood by others outside the field. In addition, the whole working world in the United States is filled with jargon about employment practices. For example, in many fields in which employees work extra hours, known as *overtime,* they may be given extra time off instead of pay. This practice is known as *comp time,* or compensatory time. When you interview an American informant about his or her work, using Questionnaire 2, it is likely that you will hear some vocabulary that is new to you, including some jargon related to the job being described. Ask your informant what these words mean and write them down. Review the following list:

To let go — to end someone's job for any reason
To fire — to let a worker go because the employer is not happy with him or her
To lay off — to let a worker go for reasons that have nothing to do with the worker, such as economic conditions
Social security — money paid by both the worker and the employer that the worker collects when he or she retires

Under the table — an illegal way of paying a worker without taking out money for taxes or social security

Workman's comp (compensation) — pay received by workers who hurt themselves on the job

Unemployment compensation ("Unemployment") — pay collected by workers for a period of months after they have been laid off

Seniority — how long each worker has been employed by the same company, compared to every other worker

Blue collar — Jobs that require physical work

White collar — office jobs

Fringe benefits (Benefits) — Money paid by the employer for employees' medical insurance, dental insurance, sick time, vacation time, etc.

Occupational hazards — health problems that can result from certain kinds of jobs

Affirmative action — a program by employers to hire more women and members of racial minority groups

Job security — protection from layoffs and firings

≡ With a Partner

1. Ask your partner to close his or her book.
2. Read half the vocabulary words above, one at a time, and ask your partner to give the definition.
3. Close your book.
4. Your partner will read the other half of the vocabulary words while you give the definitions.

ABOUT THE INTERVIEWS IN THIS CHAPTER

In your journal, you wrote about what kind of work you would like to be doing in five years. The interviews in this chapter will give you a chance to think through your plans some more and to find out more about jobs in the field that interests you.

1. In your journal, look over your own career plans. Form a group, or team, of classmates with an interest in the same general field (education, health care, business, etc.). Here are ways to form a group:

   • Your teacher can write different fields on the board and ask the class to raise their hands as each one is read aloud.
   • You could walk around the classroom until you find classmates who are interested in your field. (You can write your field on a sign and carry it around the classroom to make it easier to find others.)

2. Meet with your new *Career Team:* classmates who are interested in the same field as you. Note: If you cannot find anyone interested in the same field, form a group with others in a similar situation.

3. Choose a partner on your Career Team who shares your interests or plans. You will work with your interview partner on both Questionnaires.

Questionnaire 1: In-class

JOBS — PAST, PRESENT, AND FUTURE

With your partner, take turns interviewing each other, using the following questions. Make a few notes about each answer.

1. What kinds of jobs have you had?
2. What kind of job do you have now? *(Note: If your partner is not working now, ask about his or her last job. To do this, ask the following questions with past tense verbs written in parentheses () below. If your partner has never had a job, skip questions 3-8, and begin with question 9.)*
3. What are (were) your responsibilities? In other words, what does (did) your boss expect you to do?
4. What is (was) a typical day like for you?
5. Could you describe a typical week?
6. What do (did) you like most about the job?
7. What would you change (would you have changed) about the job if you could?
8. How did you get the job?
9. What kind of work do you see yourself doing in five years?
10. How did you decide to go into this field?
11. What will you need to do to achieve your career goals?
12. What difficulties do you think might come up for you?
13. How are you planning to deal with them?
14. How does living in the United States help with your career plans?

Signature of interview partner: _____

....

ANALYSIS WITH YOUR INTERVIEW PARTNER

1. How were your partner's experiences and plans similar to your own?
2. How were they different?

☰ With Your Partner

Talk over the ways in which your and your partner's career plans (questions 9-14) are similar and the ways in which they are different. Fill in this chart, taking turns writing down the similarities and differences in your plans.

SIMILARITIES	DIFFERENCES

2. Look over Questionnaire 2 together. You will both use it to interview someone already working in the field in which you are interested.
3. Together, brainstorm at least three additional questions to ask the informant in your field. Choose one question each that you plan to ask the person that you interview. Write it down on Questionnaire 2 next to question 13.

······················
THINK ABOUT THIS

In China, people used to call the United States "gold mountain" because of the opportunity to earn money here.

1. Do people in your native country think of the U.S. as a place where it is easy to earn lots of money?
2. In your opinion, are they correct?

≡ With a Partner from Another Country

1. Compare your answers.
2. Pretend that someone from your hometown wrote to you, asking your advice about whether or not to come to the United States to make some money. What would you tell them? Together, draft a letter of reply.

Questionnaire 2: Out-of-class

Informational Interview about Your Field of Interest

Directions: *You have already thought, written, and talked about the kind of work you would like to be doing in five years. With the help of friends, classmates, and your teacher, find someone to interview who is now working in that field. If possible, interview someone who is doing the same job that you would like to do. If you cannot find someone to interview, ask your partner if you can help interview the American informant that he or she has found. If you are both unable to find someone, your Career Team can do one interview together with an American working in your team's field of interest. If you do a group interview, be sure to divide up the questions and the note-taking.*

   Important Note: *When asking someone if they are willing to be interviewed, make sure you tell them that the purpose of the interview is* informational, *that is, to find out about their field, not to get a job. Also, explain that the information is confidential, which means that you will not name your informant in class or share the information with anyone outside of class. Write down question 13 (your own question). At the end of the interview, ask for the informant's signature and write down any new vocabulary that you learn.*

1. Could you tell me what your current job is and how long you have had it?

   _____

2. How long have you been with the same employer?

   _____

3. What are your responsibilities?

   _____

   _____

4. What is a typical day like for you?

   _____

   _____

5. Could you describe a typical week?

   _____

   _____

6. What do you like most about the job?

_____

7. What would you change about the job if you could?

_____

_____

8. How did you get the job?

_____

9. What kind of qualifications did you need to get this job?

_____

10. How did you get into this field? Do you see yourself staying?

_____

_____

11. What kind of advice would you give to someone interested in going into this field?

_____

_____

12. What is the starting pay for someone in your field? What is the top range?

_____

_____

13. Your own question.

_____

_____

Signature of informant: _____ Name: _____

☰ Analysis in Pairs

With your partner, take turns sharing information from your interview.

1. Talk about how you found someone to interview.
2. Tell how you think the interview went, including any problems you had.
3. Tell about your informant's answers to each question.
4. Talk about what it's like to get a job and to work in the United States, compared to your native countries. Is it very similar? What differences are there? Where would you prefer to work?

☰ Analysis in Career Teams

Get together in Career Teams, groups of classmates who are interested in the same field. Before answering the following questions, choose team members to do the following jobs:

- **Secretary** — will write down the answers to questions 5-7 (Make sure to write so that the reporter can read it!)
- **Reporter** — will report back to the whole class the answers to question 5-7
- **Timekeeper** — will make sure the team finishes on time
- **Discussion Leader** — will keep the discussion going and make sure everyone takes part

Take turns so that everyone in the team answers these questions:

1. What job did your informant have?
2. What advice did your informant give you?
3. What did you learn in your interview that was interesting or important for you to know in making your career plans?
4. What answers did you get to your own question (#13)?
5. What answers given by your American informant were confusing or not clear to you? Talk these over. Write down any answers (with the question number) that the group is not able to explain.
6. After everyone in the group has answered questions 1-5, make a group chart about the good points (advantages) and the negative points (disadvantages) of working in the field in which your group is interested. (See answers to questions 6 and 7 on Questionnaire 2.) If possible, write the chart on a large sheet of chart paper set up like this:

(Name of Field)	
Advantages	Disadvantages

7. Using your informants' answers to question 12, figure out the average starting pay for people in the field. Then figure out the average top salary. Write these down.

☰ Analysis in Class

After you have finished your analysis in pairs and in your Career Team, come together as a class to discuss these issues:

1. Advantages and Disadvantages of Different Fields

Listen while the reporters from each Career Team explain their team charts about the advantages and disadvantages of their field. Discuss any similarities among the different teams' charts.

2. How to Get a Job in the United States

Go to the board and write down the answer your American informant gave to question 8: "How did you get your job?" All your classmates will do the same. Return to your seat. Your teacher will cross out any answers that are repeated more than once and put a star next to the most common answers.

One student will slowly read each answer on the board aloud. After each one is read, stand up if the answer read is also a common way of getting a job in your native country. Look around the classroom to see how many classmates are also standing. Sit down. Repeat for each answer on the board.

Discuss job-hunting experiences in the United States, if any students in the class have tried to find a job. Talk about how these compare to looking for a job in other countries.

3. Understanding Informants' Confusing Answers:

Hand in any answers to Questionnaire 2 that your Career Team was not able to explain. (These were written down by the recorders in Career Teams, in answer to question 5.) Discuss these in class.

4. Job Mobility in the United States

Tally up answers to question 2 (Questionnaire 2) "How long have you been with the same employer?" by making a class line:

1. Stand up.
2. Place yourself in the class line according to how long your informant has been with the same employer.
3. Find out the median length of time that informants stayed with the same employer by counting to the middle of the line.
4. Make a class graph to represent job mobility among those interviewed. While the class stays in line, one student will fill in a graph on the blackboard using these vectors:

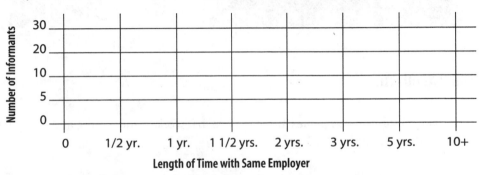

Does your data in the graph above show that Americans move around from company to company much? If they do, talk over why this might be. Do workers in other countries tend to spend more or less time with the same employer? Discuss these answers, connecting them to the importance of the values of *individualism* and *loyalty*.

5. **Rates of Pay**

   The recorders from each Career Team will write down the name of each field on the board. Guess which field has the highest pay.

   Find out how good your guess was after the recorders from the Career Teams write on the board the actual average top salary calculated by each team. Rank the fields according to pay.

   Talk about what the differences in pay among fields says about American values.

   Discuss whether these fields are ranked the same by pay in other countries. For example, is the highest-paying field also the highest-paying in other countries from which members of the class come?

THINK ABOUT THIS

In many American companies, there is a rule that workers must retire at the age of 65. Do you agree with this policy?

≡ Take Sides

1. Stand up and go to one side of the room if you agree, the other side if you disagree. (Your teacher will indicate the sides.)
2. Pair up with someone on your side of the room and talk over the reasons that you feel the way you do.
3. With everyone else who chose the same side, make a list of reasons to support your side. Write them down.
4. Be prepared to state the list of reasons that was put together by your side. The side with the best list of reasons will win.

JOURNAL

How have your career plans changed after doing the work in this chapter? Do you feel better or worse about your plans? Explain. What have you realized you will have to do in order to be successful in your field? Have you thought about other fields after learning more about them?

Additional Activities

PREPARING A RESUMÉ

Prepare a draft of your resumé. Go over it with a partner. Have a native English speaker check it. Then type it. Make several photocopies. Pass it to the classmates in your Career Group and get their suggestions for ways to make it better.

Sample:

Ping An

Address:
   32 West Lake Street, Bridgewater, CA 95034

Telephone:
   325-743-8902 (evenings)

Social Security:
   733-49-2231 (This information is optional.)

Education:

> 1990- present
>> English Language Training Program, Bridgewater, CA
>
> 1989-90
>> Bridgewater High School, Bridgewater, CA
>> Degree granted: High School General Diploma
>
> 1985-89
>> High School for Girls, Taipei, Taiwan

Work Experience:

> 1989-present
>> Waitress, Lucky Garden Restaurant, 89 High Street, Paxton, CA.
>> Responsibilities: wait on tables
>
> 1990-91
>> Tutor in after-school program (volunteer, part-time).
>> Community After-Care, 72 Grove St., Bridgewater, CA.
>> Responsibilities: design and implement tutoring plan for three junior high students.

Special Skills:

> Fluent in Chinese (Mandarin)

References available on request.

···

DEALING WITH JOB DISCRIMINATION

≡ Think about This

Looking back at the Case Study at the beginning of the chapter, what if Toan's fears about the company's discriminating against Vietnamese were correct? Pretend that Toan did not get the job, and that Hien overheard her boss asking a Caucasian coworker, "Do you have any friends who want a position in programming? I think the company already has enough Asians in the programming department."

1. What do you think Hien should do?
2. What do you think Toan should do?
3. If you need to know about the laws against employment discrimination in the United States, get a copy of the equal employment opportunity policy at a local employer such as your school, or make a telephone call to the state, town, or federal agency responsible for dealing with discrimination cases.

≡ **In a Group**

1. Work out a solution to the racial discrimination in the computer company.
2. Role-play your solution for the class.

....
JOB OPPORTUNITIES IN THE NEWSPAPER

Most Sunday newspapers list jobs in the Classified or Help Wanted section. Skim through the ads on Sunday to find out the answers to the following questions. Write down your answers and any abbreviations used in the ads that you do not understand. Ask your teacher to explain them.

1. What job advertised offers the highest pay?
2. What job advertised offers the lowest pay?
3. What job advertised requires no experience?
4. What fields have the most job listings?
5. What job requires or prefers fluency in another language?
6. What job offers flexible or part-time hours?
7. Find three jobs in the field in which you are interested and write down the qualifications needed.

Chapter 6

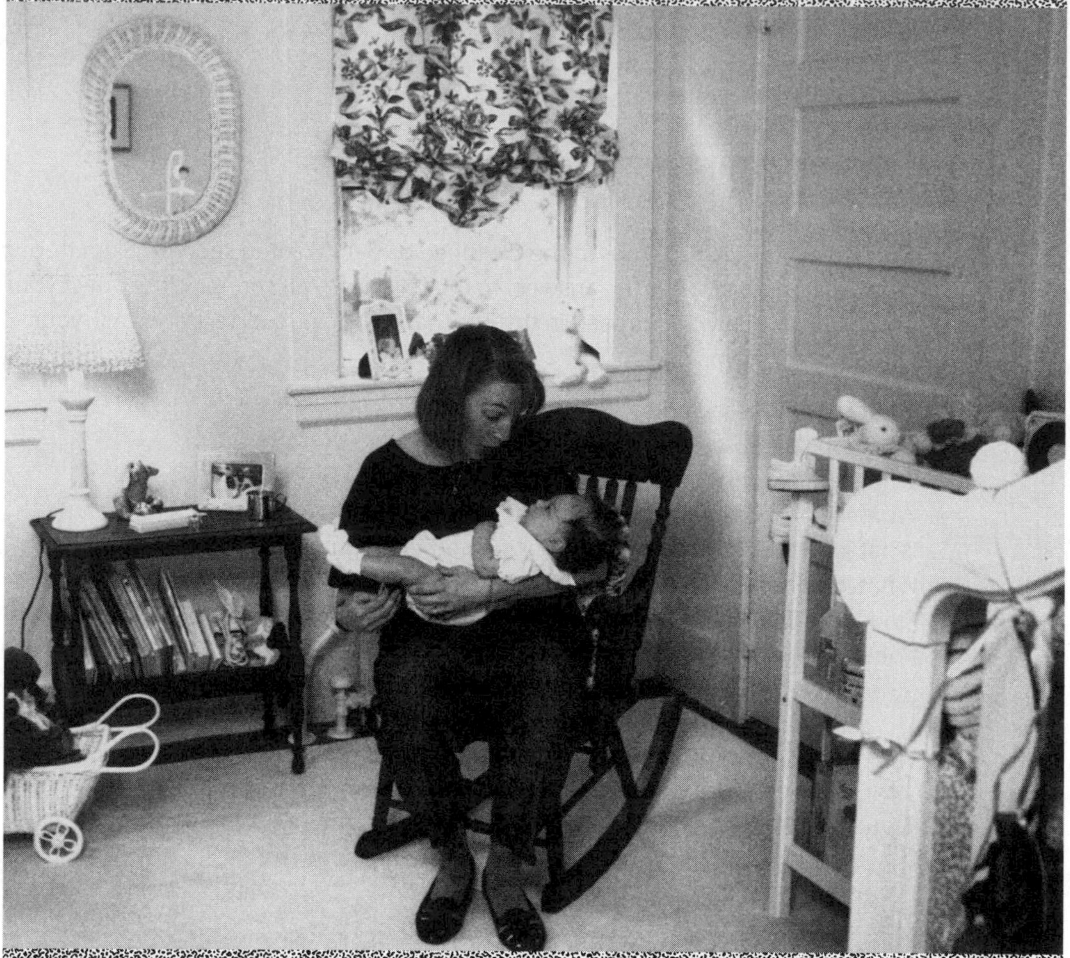

Warm-up

Most American parents believe that it is best for each child to have his or her own bedroom. Babies in the United States usually sleep alone in their own little beds, which are called cribs. So American children learn from the very beginning to become independent from their parents.

1. Where did you sleep as a baby?
2. Where will your own babies sleep?
3. Why?
4. Did you have your own room as a child? How did you feel about that?

☰ With a Partner

1. Compare your answers to the questions above.
2. Talk over this question: How does the place in which a baby sleeps affect what kind of adult he or she becomes, if at all?

☰ As a Class

1. Find out the class' responses to question 1 above: Where did you sleep as a baby?
2. Make a bar graph on the board that shows the class' answers.
3. Talk over the family values reflected in these answers.

JOURNAL

Families all around the world are alike in certain basic ways. What are they? Name at least five things that all families do. Then write about some of the ways American families seem to do things differently from families in your native culture.

Preparation

....

CASE STUDY

Rosa, a Mexican-American college student, and Annie, a student from an Anglo-American family, were roommates at an American university. They shared a small dormitory room and got along very well — until a problem came up.

One day Rosa said to Annie, "My cousin wants to come see the college. She's thinking about going to school here next year, and she wants to check out dorm life. Do you mind if she stays with us while she visits?"

Annie answered, "Gee, it's pretty crowded with just the two of us. Things will be awful tight. Where's she going to sleep?"

"Oh, that's no problem. She can sleep in my bed with me."

"Well, OK," said Annie. "It's up to you."

"You're a doll, Annie," answered Rosa. "She'll be here tomorrow."

A week later Rosa's cousin was still with them. Rosa paid for all her meals and missed some of her classes so that she could help her cousin find her way around. Rosa never complained about any of this, but it bothered Annie, so she decided to have a word with her friend.

"Rosa," she said. "I know it's none of my business, but I don't like to see someone walking all over you. It's not fair for your cousin to take advantage of your time and your money like this. You have your own life to live, and after all, she's only your second cousin. You can't even get a decent night's sleep!"

Rosa was surprised. She answered, "Oh, the bed doesn't bother me. It reminds me of sleeping with my sister as a child. You're right, though, about letting my work go. I know I'm cutting too many classes, but family comes first. I just couldn't leave my cousin here to be on her own. Her father and my mother grew up together, and he and my dad work together. I don't mind helping her out. But if she's bothering you, I can find out when she's planning to leave."

Even after their conversation, Annie could not understand the change in her roommate. Before the visit from her cousin, Rosa had always seemed like such an independent, responsible person. She never missed a class and was totally committed to her studies. Now she seemed ready to throw everything out the window for the sake of a distant relative.

GLOSSARY FOR VOCABULARY IN CASE STUDY

Dormitory — student housing owned and run by colleges (dorm — abbreviation)
Check out — to see for oneself

Awful — very; slang for "awfully"

Tight — crowded, close

Doll — a wonderful, generous female (colloquial)

To complain — To say that something is wrong

To have a word with — to speak to someone about something specific

None of my business — not my affair; nothing to do with me

Walk all over — to exploit, take advantage of

Cut classes — to miss classes without permission

Responsible — someone who always does what they are supposed to do (responsibilities — duties; what one is supposed to do)

(To be) committed to — (To) give much importance to

Throw out the window — to lose something, to let an opportunity go

≡ Questions for Discussion

1. Why did Annie think that Rosa had changed?
2. Why did Rosa feel that she had to help her cousin out?
3. Do you think Annie's ideas are typical of American culture?
4. Do you think Rosa's ideas are typical of any other cultures?
5. What would you do if you were Rosa?
6. What would you do if you were Annie?

THINK ABOUT THIS

A wedding brings two families together. It is also a time for family members to see each other.

1. When was the last time that your family all got together?

≡ With a Partner

1. Tell each other about the last time your family got together.
2. Do you look forward to family occasions or not? Explain.

....
BACKGROUND READING

One reason why Annie and Rosa did not understand each other is because of different cultural values around the meaning of family. Though both students were Americans, family meant something to Rosa, a Mexican-American, that it did not mean to Annie, whose ideas were typical of the dominant American culture, especially in Anglo-American families. Like many Hispanics, Rosa felt that "family comes first," meaning that her own individual needs came second. That point of view was hard for Annie to understand, because in the dominant American culture the individual's needs are often seen as more important. In Annie's view, Rosa was being weak and irresponsible to let her cousin's needs come before her own. For Rosa, family responsibilities were more important than her school responsibilities.

The dominant American culture puts great pressure on young people of college age to be independent from their families. The value of independence, in fact, is first learned in the family. American parents try to teach independence from the beginning of a child's life. Independence is the reason why parents let their babies feed themselves just as soon as they can and begin to make decisions for themselves almost as soon as they can talk. Most American parents feel that they have done their job well if their children are able to live on their own in their twenties. In some other cultures, family members tend to depend on each other more, and this mutual dependence, known as *interdependence,* is seen as positive, not negative. Most Asian and Hispanic cultures, for example, value interdependence more than independence.

Because of these different cultural values, it is sometimes difficult for people to understand and accept family relationships in other cultures. People from Hispanic and Asian backgrounds may feel that Anglo-American families are cold and distant, because of the independence of the family members. On the other hand, Anglo-Americans like Annie may feel that family life among other cultural groups is too close for comfort and makes individual growth more difficult.

Another reason why Annie was not able to understand Rosa and her cousin was because family is defined differently in the two cultures. If you ask Anglo-Americans if they come from a large family, they will tell you the number of brothers and sisters they have. They think of family as the nuclear family: parents and their children. The rest of the family is known as the *extended* family, and Anglo-Americans generally have less contact with extended family members than do people from some other backgrounds. Annie probably did not even know her second cousins. In other cultures where people move around less, the extended family is far more important than it is in the United States, where nuclear families often live far away from grandparents. Many Americans do not feel much family responsibility toward aunts, uncles, and cousins. Because of this, Annie might have understood Rosa if she had spent so much time with a brother or sister, rather than with "just" a second cousin.

In Rosa's culture, there is not such a big difference between nuclear and extended family responsibilities. For many Hispanics, Asians, Africans, and Arabs, the extended family is very important in childrearing, in social life, and in caring for older people. In these societies, the extended family is the main financial and emotional support for people in times of crisis. This is not so for most Americans, who rely more on friends, institutions, and professionals.

GLOSSARY FOR BACKGROUND READING VOCABULARY

Dominant — majority; most powerful

Anglo-American — of English-American background

Hispanic — people from Spanish-speaking Latin-American countries, or from Latin-American backgrounds, who live in the United States

To put pressure on — to push; to demand; to squeeze

Mutual — shared; including both people

Too close for comfort — so close that it feels uncomfortable

Extended family — aunts, uncles, grandparents, cousins, etc; all relatives outside the nuclear family

Childrearing — bringing up, raising, or caring for children from childhood to adulthood

Crisis — a serious difficulty or problem

To rely on — to go to for help; to count on someone's support

≡ Pair Work

1. Draw your family tree. Next to each relative, write his or her name and relationship to you — *in your native language AND in English* (for example, CHI-KUANG CHEN, grandfather).

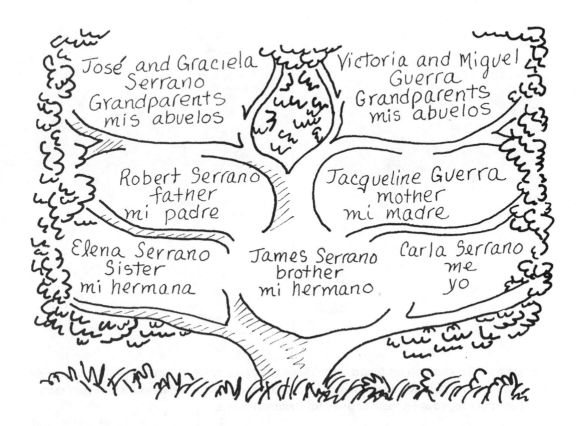

2. Draw a circle around your *nuclear family.*
3. Put a check mark next to every relationship term in your native language that does not have an exact translation in English.
4. Explain your family tree to a partner.
5. Explain the terms that do not translate. Discuss why that may be.
6. Ask each other this question: "Before you moved to the United States, how often did you see each person on your family tree?" Decide if your answers mean that your family is more focused on the *nuclear* or on the *extended* family.
7. Talk over with your partner the ways that your family taught you to be independent when you were growing up — if they did. Then discuss how you were encouraged to depend on family and to take care of your family's needs. Fill in the chart below with examples from the lives of both you and your partner. Put a star next to the best example of independence and a star next to the best example of interdependence.

INDEPENDENCE	INTERDEPENDENCE
Example: I was sent to the store alone.	*Example:* I walked my sister to school.

8. On a similar chart on the board, write down the items by which you and your partner put a star. Other pairs will do the same. Discuss among your classmates whether your families encouraged *independence* or *interdependence* more.

"Pops, can you hear me?"

....
THINK ABOUT THIS

Who is the person in the photo talking to?

≡ With a Partner

1. Compare answers to the above question. Check with another pair if you are not sure.
2. Who would you expect the person in the photo to be talking to if you overheard her saying:

   a. Granny
   b. Aunt Mabel
   c. Mom
   d. Honey
   e. Uncle Fred
   f. Gramps
   g. Great-grandma
   h. Nana

3. Except for parents, grandparents, uncles, and aunts, most Americans call all their other relatives by their first, or given, names. Is this true in your native language? If not, explain to your partner what you call the members of your family.

Interviews and Analysis

 INTERVIEW TIP: UNDERSTANDING PHRASES ABOUT FAMILY LIFE

Americans often use expressions about family and family relationships that cannot always be found in a dictionary. To help you better understand what your American informant is saying, study these definitions first:

Baby-sitter: A person who is paid to take care of children, usually in the children's home. *To baby-sit (for) is the verb. (Example: Sina helped the children with their homework when she baby-sat for them after school.)*

Black sheep: A family member who is different from the rest of the family in some way — often in a way that the family does not approve of. *(Since she went to live in Europe against her parents' wishes, she was the black sheep in the family.)*

Blended family: A nuclear family formed by remarriage, including children from one or more previous marriages. *(It took Kim a while to get used to having stepbrothers and a stepfather in her new blended family.)*

Child abuse: Physical, sexual, or mental mistreatment of children by adults, usually family members. *(There are many more reports of child abuse due to drug use in the United States since crack cocaine became popular.)*

Common-law Marriage/Husband/Wife: A family in which both parents live together but have never gotten married. *(Mr. Suarez has a common-law wife whom he has been with for 17 years.)*

Day Care: A place at which children and babies too young to be in school are taken care of, usually by people not related to them. *(Carla had a hard time finding good day care for her daughter when she decided to go back to work.)*

Distant relatives: Family members not closely related, such as second cousins and great aunts and uncles. *(When Theresa visited Italy, she met some of her husband's distant cousins.)*

Dual-career family: A family in which both husband and wife hold paying jobs. *(Many more schools today have after-school programs for students, because there are so many dual-career families.)*

Generation gap: Misunderstanding or conflict between parents and children, from adolescence on. *(Vinh was sure that the generation gap in his family was wider because his parents followed the traditional Vietnamese customs.)*

Godparents: When a child is baptized in some Christian churches, one or two adults are chosen by the parents to have a special relationship with the child. *(Tommy's godmother always takes him out to eat on his birthday.)*

Immediate family: Nuclear family; parents and their children. *(Bill and Noriko decided to have a very small wedding and only invite their immediate families.)*

Latchkey child: A child who stays at home alone after school (idiom). *(The number of latchkey children has increased as more American women have taken jobs.)*

Nursery school/ Preschool: A program for 3- and 4-year-old children to prepare them for school. *(Oanh is learning how to get along with other children at nursery school.)*

Nursing home: An institution set up to take care of elderly people who cannot take care of themselves. *(After Bob's grandmother died, the family decided that his grandfather needed to go into a nursing home.)*

Only child: A child without brothers or sisters. *(Although he was an only child, Peter's parents did not spoil him.)*

Retirement center: A place in which older people can live on their own with support when they need it. *(Mr. and Mrs. Nucci found it was too much for them to take care of their house after Mr. Nucci's heart attack, so they sold it and entered a retirement center.)*

Single-parent: A mother or father who raises a child or children alone, due to divorce, death, or other reasons. *(Single-parent families used to be called "broken homes," a phrase which is not used much anymore.)*

Social security: Money that American workers and their employers pay the government, which is returned to the workers when they retire. *(Mr. Chin retired to Florida when he was 65, living on his social security checks, the pension from his job, and the money he got from the sale of his house.)*

☰ Practice with a Partner

1. Take turns reading the above definitions and sentences out loud.
2. After each one is read, talk about how it applies to your native culture. *Example:* "In Peru, most families have relatives take care of their children instead of hiring baby-sitters. Wealthy families have full-time servants to do childcare, called *niñeras."*

Questionnaire 1: In-class

FAMILY LIFE

Choose an interview partner who has the same (or almost the same) number of siblings (brothers and sisters) that you have. Interview each other, using the following questionnaire. When it is your turn to be interviewed, try to use at least three of the vocabulary words about family life that were introduced in the previous section. After you have interviewed your partner, tell him or her which responses you found most interesting.

1. Tell me your full name and how it was chosen.
2. When you were a child, who lived with you?
3. When you were a child, who took care of you when your parents were not home?
4. When you were growing up, what were the responsibilities of each child in the house?

5. As you were growing up, how did your parents feel about their children becoming independent? Give examples.
6. What was family life like in your home when you were a teenager? What was it like when you disagreed with your parents?
7. In your culture, where do young adults live before they get married? Why?
8. In your culture, what do people think of a 27-year-old person who lives at home with his or her parents? Explain.
9. Nowadays, when you have a problem, who do you go to for help? Is that typical in your culture?
10. In your culture, where do older people live, and what money do they live on?
11. When does your whole family get together?
12. How do people in your extended family depend on each other or help each other out?

Signature of interview partner: _____

Native country: _____

≡ With Your Interview Partner

After you have finished interviewing each other, talk over your own ideas about how to raise a family. Using the questionnaire as a guide, discuss whether you plan to raise your own children the same way that your parents raised you, or whether you plan to do things differently.

WANTED: 1 M/F nonsmoker to share 3 BDRM apt. in CLARK. Lg yard, frplce, sunny. Nr. bus. $325+ utilities. 523-4573 (eve)

WESTVALE prof F seeks same to share 2 BDRM apt. Must be neat quiet nonsmkr. Avl. 5/22. Free pkg. $275+ 522-7893.

THINK ABOUT THIS

Young American adults who leave home often have trouble finding affordable housing. One solution is to live with *roommates* (to share an apartment, not necessarily a bedroom) or *housemates* (to share a house). Advertisements like the two above, posted on community bulletin boards, are one way to find a place to live and people with whom to share housing expenses.

Look over these advertisements and then read the following statements about them. Some of the statements are *opinions,* while others are *facts.* Some of the facts are true and others are false. Decide which are facts and which are opinions:

1. The apartment in Clark is more expensive than the one in Westvale.
2. Only the Clark apartment includes utilities.
3. It would be safer to live in the Westvale apartment if you are female.
4. The Clark apartment is nicer.
5. The people who wrote these ads don't mind living with strangers.
6. Roommates are common in the U.S. because American families are not close.

≡ With a Partner

1. Talk over which statements are opinions and which are facts (whether true or false). Write an "O" next to the opinions and a "F" next to the facts.
2. Write down three more statements about the ads, including facts and opinions. Give these to another pair to mark with "O" or "F."
3. Get together with the other pair and go over all your answers together, including statements 1-6 above. Together, think of one *opinion* about family life in the United States, and one *fact* or observation.

≡ In Class

1. Write your group's two statements of fact and opinion about American family life on the board. Read the statements that other groups wrote.
2. Talk over the importance of separating facts and opinions when trying to understand another culture.
3. Discuss some opinions about American family life that are held by people in your culture. On what facts are these opinions based? Do you agree?

Questionnaire 2: Out-of-class

AMERICAN FAMILY LIFE

Interview an American informant about family life in the United States and take notes on his or her answers. Make up one question of your own and write down any new vocabulary you hear.

1. Tell me your full name and how it was chosen.

_____

_____

_____

2. When you were growing up, who lived with you?

_____

_____

3. When you were a child, who took care of you when your parents were not home?

_____

4. When you were growing up, what were the responsibilities of each child in the house?

_____

_____

_____

5. As you were growing up, how did your parents feel about their children becoming independent? Give examples.

_____

_____

_____

6. What was family life like when you were a teenager? What was it like when you disagreed with your parents?

_____

_____

_____

_____

7. Where do young American adults live before they get married? Why?

_____

_____

_____

8. In the United States, what do most people think of a 27-year-old person who lives at home with his or her parents?

_____

_____

9. Nowadays, when you have a problem, who do you go to for help? Would that be typical for most Americans?

_____

_____

10. In your culture, where do older people live and what money do they live on?

_____

_____

11. When does your whole family get together?

_____

12. What are the ways that people in your extended family depend on each other or help each other out?

_____

_____

13. Your own question.

_____

_____

Signature of American informant interviewed: _____ Sex: _____

Place of birth: _____ Age: _____ Ethnic background: _____

Parents' work: _____

New vocabulary: _____

ANALYSIS WITH YOUR INTERVIEW PARTNER

1. Talk over how your interviews with American informants went. Discuss any difficulties or problems that you had and help each other come up with possible solutions for next time.
2. Discuss which answers given by your American informant surprised you the most.
3. Discuss which answers you thought were typically American.
4. In what ways did the American informant's family remind you of your own family?
5. Talk about what you would have liked about growing up in the family described by your American informant.
6. What do you think you would *not* have liked about growing up in that family?
7. What answers did your American informant give that helped you to better understand the value that Americans place on independence? Were there any ways that your informant's family also valued interdependence?
8. Write down any answers that you did not understand.

ANALYSIS IN GROUPS OF FOUR

With your interview partner, find another pair of interview partners to form a group of four. Choose as the group **secretary** the student who interviewed the oldest informant. The secretary will be responsible for writing down the group's answers to questions 2, 3, and 4. Whoever interviewed the youngest informant will be the group **reporter,** sharing the group's answers with the whole class later on. The other two members of the group can choose who will be the **timekeeper** and who will be the **quiet captain,** to make sure that the group does not get too noisy.

1. Take turns telling a little bit about who you interviewed: age, background, what their family was like, etc. Do not use full names.
2. Share answers to question 13, the extra question.
3. As a group, answer this question: What are the ways in which family life teaches Americans to become independent? List at least four ways.
4. Briefly share the answers that your informants gave to each question on the questionnaire. The secretary will write down the most common answer for each question.

ANALYSIS IN CLASS

1. Make a class summary of the most common answers to Questionnaire 2. For each question, the reporters will read off the most common answer collected by their group of four. Two class secretaries will fill in the following chart on the board: One will write the most common answer to each question, and the other will write an answer that several other informants gave.

Most common American answer	Other answers
1.	
2.	
3.	
4.	
5.	
6.	
7.	
8.	
9.	
10.	
11.	
12.	

2. Which of the common American answers listed on the board chart show how the nuclear family is more important than the extended family in American life? As each question number is read aloud by one of the class secretaries, raise your hand if you think that answer shows the importance of the nuclear family.

3. Look over the "other answers" given by Americans listed above. Some of the differences in Americans' answers may be explained by their age, sex, social class, or ethnic background. For example, it is more common for young Americans from working-class homes to live at home until marriage than it is for children in middle or upper-class families. Discuss whether some of the "other" answers can be explained by informants' age, gender, social class or ethnic background?

4. Reporters will go to the board and write the four ways that their group found that Americans teach independence to their children. As each one is read out loud by the reporter, stand up if you think it is a good idea, that is, if it is a practice that you would use in your own family.

JOURNAL

When people move to the United States from other parts of the world to raise their families, parents and children sometimes have problems because of cultural differences. From what you have learned about the differences in family life in the United States and in other cultures, write about what some of these problems might be. First, write about the problems that a parent from another culture might have trying to raise children in the United States. Then write about the problems from the point of view of American-born children whose parents come from another culture.

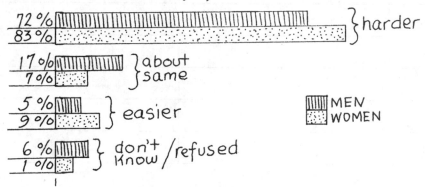

Family Life

Do you think it's easier or harder for parents to raise children now than it was when your parents were raising you?

72% / 83% } harder

17% / 7% } about same

5% / 9% } easier

[[[[MEN
[::] WOMEN

6% / 1% } don't know /refused

THINK ABOUT THIS

According to an American newspaper poll of 400 parents, 78% thought that it was harder to raise children today than when they were growing up.

1. What do you think some of their reasons were?
2. Why do you think 11% more women agreed than men?

≡ **Take a Stand**

1. Stand up.
2. If you agree that it is harder today to raise children, go to one side of the room with all your classmates who feel the same way. If you think it is about the same, go to another side of the room. If you think that it is easier, go stand near the door with other classmates who agree.
3. With those classmates who agree with you, make a list of your reasons why. Appoint a secretary to write them down.
4. Someone from your group will read off your list to the other groups. Before returning to your seat, count the number of students in each group and figure out if the opinions were similar in percentages to those in the poll in the graph above.

Additional Activities

....
ROLE-PLAY

With a partner, role-play the conflict between Annie and Rosa. Act out a solution that helps them to understand each other. Perform it for another pair, then watch as they act it out for you. Sit down with the other pair and choose one of the following family situations. Talk over how to act it out two different ways: as it would happen in an American family and as it would happen in a family from another culture. Perform for another group of four or in front of the whole class.

1. You have just graduated from college. You and your parents have different ideas about where you should live. How do you present your ideas to your parents and how do they respond?
2. Your grandfather has just died. Your family meets to talk about how to take care of your grandmother. What do they say and what do they decide?
3. You have a new job. Your sister calls you at work one day to tell you that she is very ill. She lives about eight hours away. What do you decide to do and what do you tell your boss?
4. Your brother, who is in high school, has just been caught drinking beer. One of his teachers calls your parents. How does your family react?

WRITING ASSIGNMENT

How has family life in your native culture changed since your parents were young? Write a paragraph on the most important changes since your parents were children. First, brain-storm about the topic, using the idea map below. Think about how family recreation has changed, for example, then make notes in the circle below. Fill in the blank circles with other areas of family life that have changed

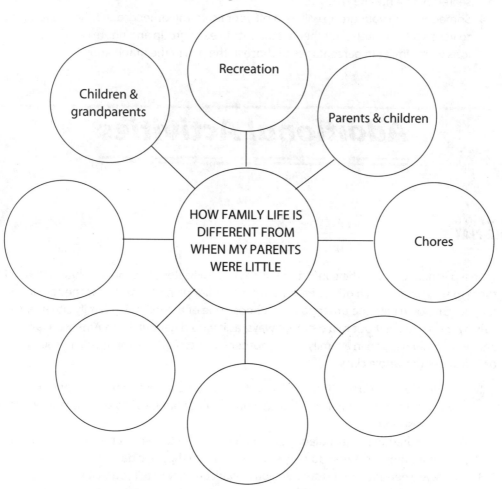

Begin the paragraph with this topic sentence: "There have been several important changes in _____ family life since my parents were children." (country)

Begin the next sentence with "First of all ..." and continue by explaining one of the ideas that you filled in on a circle on the idea map above. Continue by writing about another change from the idea map, beginning the sentence with "Secondly ..." When you have written about all the ideas that you want to include, write a concluding sentence stating your opinion about these changes.

. . . .
FIELD TRIP

With a group from your class, make a visit to a day-care center. Call first and explain that the purpose of your visit is to learn about day care in the United States. When you get there, divide the group up. Have each of these groups choose a different teacher and adult to observe, or study, carefully. Take notes on these issues: What does the child do with other children? What and how does the adult try to "teach" the child? (Pay attention to nonverbal communication too!)

Afterward, get together with your group. First, write a thank-you note to the day-care center. Next, share your observations of individual children and adults together. If anyone is familiar with day-care centers in other countries, compare them. Together, prepare a chart to present to the class about the advantages and disadvantages of day-care centers, based on your visit and discussion.

Chapter 7

Warm-up

THINK ABOUT THIS

Who has it better, males or females?
   Note: "To have it better" is an idiom that means to have a better or easier time in life.

☰ Take Sides

1. Decide whether you think males or females have it better. Choose one reason why.
2. Stand up and go to one side of the room with everyone in the class who feels the same way.
3. Listen to the reasons given by everyone on your side and then share yours. Get a recorder to make a list of all the reasons why people on your side feel that males (or females) have it better. Appoint a reporter to read the list to the other side.
4. If your group chooses "males have it better," vote on this question: Do males have it better in the United States or in your native country? If your group chose "females have it better," vote on this question: Do females have it better in the United States or in your native country? With the others on your side, compare this issue in your native country and in the United States.
5. Go back to your seat. Listen while the two reporters present the list of reasons prepared by each side.

JOURNAL

What have you noticed about American males and females that is different from what you are used to? Describe some of the differences that you have noticed. Write about how you feel about them.

Preparation

....
"DOWN/UP" IDIOMS

Before reading the Case Study, skim through it and copy every sentence that has the word *up* or *down* in it. Read over the definitions in the glossary for *up* and *down* idioms. If the sentences that you copied have either *up* or *down* used as idioms or as slang, write a check-mark after the sentence.

> *Examples:* 1. Then she looked down.
> 2. What's up? ✓

When you have finished, take turns with a partner reading each sentence that you checked off out loud. After reading each sentence, repeat it without using *down* or *up*. Instead, substitute a word or expression that means the same thing.

> *Example:* What's up? *Say:* "What's happening?"

....
CASE STUDY

As partners in chemistry lab, Ron and Yem Ling made a good team. Yem Ling already had a background in chemistry, having studied it in Chinese back home, and Ron was able to help out with some of the English terms that Yem Ling did not understand. By the middle of the semester, the two had become friends. When they had lab together on Mondays, they often chatted about the movies that they had each seen over the weekend. Yem Ling especially was up on all the latest films.

One Monday Ron and Yem Ling were discussing a film that each had seen over the weekend. Ron had loved it and Yem Ling had not liked it at all. They got into such a hot debate over the film that they had to hurry up in order to finish their chemistry experiment before the end of class.

As they were cleaning up, Ron teased Yem Ling: "I know why you're so down on the movie, girl. It was over your head. You just didn't get it."

Yem Ling tapped Ron on the arm, pretending to hit him. Ron laughed and said, "Whoa, calm down. I'm sorry. I didn't mean to put you down. But I think that if you saw the film again and thought about what I said, you'd see what I mean. In fact, why don't we check it out again together this weekend. How about Saturday night? Or maybe if you're not up for seeing it again, we could catch another movie."

Yem Ling waited a moment before answering. Then she said, "I don't think so, Ron. Sorry."

Ron said, "Well, maybe some other time."

Yem Ling smiled and looked down at the floor.

After class, Ron ran into his old friend Phil. "Hey, Ron. What's up?"

Ron explained that Yem Ling had turned him down for a date. "I just don't get it, Phil," he said. "It's really getting me down. Yem Ling and I really have a great time together. She's always up for a laugh. I *think* she likes me, but maybe not. Maybe she's just leading me on. Or maybe she's seeing someone. But that doesn't make any sense, because she says she goes out to the movies with her girlfriend every Saturday night. I just can't figure out what's going on."

"That's easy," teased Phil, as he slapped his friend on the back. "It's your ugly face."

GLOSSARY FOR VOCABULARY USED IN CASE STUDY

Chat — to talk, usually in a friendly, casual, and informal way

To be up on — to know a lot about (idiom)

Tease — to bother in a friendly way

To be down on — to dislike; to be unhappy with (slang)

To get it — to understand (slang)

Over your head — too difficult for you; on too high a level (idiom)

Calm down — get calm; calm yourself (idiom)

To put somebody down — to insult someone; to disrespect someone (slang)

Check it out — see it (slang)

To be up for — to want to, to be in the mood for (slang)

To catch a movie — to see a movie (slang)

What's up? — What's new, or what's happening? (slang)

To turn down — to say no; to refuse (idiom)

To get someone down — to make someone unhappy (slang)

To be up for a laugh — to have a good sense of humor; to be open to jokes (slang)

To lead someone on — to act in a false way; to act in a way that you do not mean, especially about liking someone (idiom)

To see someone — to be dating someone or be romantically involved (idiom)

☰ With a Partner of the Opposite Sex (if possible)

Talk over the following questions and try to think of several answers that might be true for each. Then take turns writing down two possible answers for each question.

1. Why did Phil say that Ron had an ugly face?
2. Did Yem Ling like Ron? Explain.
3. Why did Yem Ling say no when Ron asked her to the movies?
4. How does Ron feel?
5. How does Yem Ling feel?
6. Will Ron ask Yem Ling out again? Explain.
7. Will she accept? Explain.

THINK ABOUT THIS

In English, people in love often call each other names that refer to sweet things to eat. Some of the most common are *sweetie, honey, sugar, sweetie pie.* These are known as *terms of affection* or *terms of endearment,* or sometimes *pet names.*

1. In your native language, do lovers call each other names of sweet food too?
2. Write down a list of the most common names that people in love call each other in your native language. Translate the list into English.

☰ Cut It Out

1. Cut out an index card or a small piece of paper in the shape of a heart. (This is easier if you fold the paper in half first.)
2. Choose your favorite word from the list you made. Write it on your heart in English and then in your native language. Decorate the heart if you like.

☰ Put It Up

1. Tape your small heart onto a very large sheet of heart-shaped paper (provided by your teacher). Your classmates will do the same. Your teacher will put up the poster on the wall.
2. Read what you wrote to your classmates and explain anything that they do not understand. Listen to your classmates while they explain their hearts to you.
3. Make another poster with English terms of endearment such as Honey and Cupcake written on the hearts. Find out more pet names from Americans you know. Make more hearts and put them up.

BACKGROUND READING

In all human relationships, it is impossible to know for sure what is going on in the other person's mind. Often, open communication seems to be even more of a problem between males and females. Ron, for example, was having difficulty understanding what Yem Ling's "no" was really all about. Did she really not like him? Did she already have a boyfriend? Did she just say no when she really meant yes so that she would not appear to be too eager and available? Understanding the real meaning of a woman's "no" has often been a problem for men throughout history. Misunderstandings can be much more serious than what happened between Ron and Yem Ling. For example, the American public is beginning to realize that the crime of "date rape" is somewhat common. Date rape happens when a person does not believe that his or her date really means "no" when he or she says it and forces that person to have sex.

As tricky as male-female relationships can be in any culture, things seem to get even more complicated in cross-cultural situations. Often, people are not even aware of the cultural dimension of misunderstandings. When Ron talked over his problem with his friend Phil, for example, he did not even question whether Yem Ling's Chinese background had anything to do with her refusal to date him. He assumed that Yem Ling was free to go out on a casual date with whomever she wanted. This assumption may not necessarily be true for a daughter in a traditional Asian family. In such a family, the American custom of dating many people before marriage may not be accepted, and daughters are expected to do what their family believes is right, even if they disagree.

Ron's invitation, typical of American dating customs, was based on a number of American cultural assumptions. Basic cultural assumptions are beliefs about human nature and how the world works. One assumption that is very strong in American culture is that marriages work out best when people marry for love. Therefore, Americans believe that families should have little to say about who their children marry. Another American cultural assumption is the belief that love can overcome any differences in backgrounds, as in the popular expression, "Love conquers all." Yet another American cultural assumption is the belief that dating is good practice for marriage. Dating is seen as necessary practice in forming relationships with the opposite sex. Americans believe that if partners have no experience in romantic relationships, they will not be well prepared for marriage. These American beliefs or assumptions help explain dating and marriage customs. They also strongly reflect the all-important American value of individualism, especially the importance of individual happiness.

Traditional Chinese cultural assumptions about finding a marriage partner are completely different. They reflect traditional Chinese values that place family needs above the happiness of the individual. Therefore, in traditional Chinese families, the desires of the individual are far less important in choosing a marriage partner than are the opinions of the family. This custom also reflects the traditional Chinese belief that older people know more than younger people. Although things are changing in many parts of Asia, in more rural regions parents continue to play an active role in deciding who their children should marry.

Traditional Chinese cultural assumptions about what makes a marriage work are different from Western beliefs. Family harmony, rather than individual happiness, is the marriage ideal. In Chinese tradition, harmony is achieved by following Confucian teachings about obligation and respect. Within the Confucian value system, wives are taught to obey and respect their husbands, just as children are taught to obey and respect their parents. Again, these ideas have been challenged in recent times, especially in urban areas; however, the traditions are thousands of years old.

In the case study, nothing is said about Yem Ling's parents, except that they are Chinese immigrants. Thus, it is quite possible that they simply did not allow her to date at all. Then why did she say nothing about this to Ron? She may not have told Ron this out of embarrassment or out of a desire to save face for her family. There is also another possible explanation why Yem Ling would not go out with Ron. It is possible that her family did not want her to date a Caucasian because they feared that their daughter might not marry a Chinese man. Some Chinese families feel that it is so important to have Chinese grandchildren that they strongly discourage their children from dating non-Chinese. It is feared that Chinese traditions will not be continued if children intermarry with non-Chinese. Another reason why many immigrant parents fear intermarriage is because they fear that their children may be exposed to racism if they marry outside their race.

Of course, it is impossible to tell from the case study exactly what was really going on in Yem Ling's mind. Maybe she just doesn't like Ron. But it would be a mistake not to consider that the cultural assumptions, values, and traditions of her family might be important.

GLOSSARY FOR BACKGROUND READING VOCABULARY

Tricky — complicated; not easy; requiring care
Cross-cultural — comparing two or more cultures
Dimension — level
Refusal — the act of saying no
Assume, assumption — believe or think something is true; belief, idea

Human nature — how people behave
Conquer — overcome; be stronger than
Harmony — smooth relations; lack of conflict; when everyone gets along
Confucian — an ancient Chinese philosophy, based on the teachings of Confucius
Obey — listen to; act according to one's wishes
Save face — save from shame; avoid embarrassment
Caucasian — the "white" race
Discourage — make it difficult; try to prevent
Intermarry — to marry outside one's religion or race

☰ Questions for Discussion

1. Basic cultural assumptions are what people in a society believe to be true. According to the Background Reading, what are two American cultural assumptions about dating and marriage?
2. According to the Background Reading, what are two traditional Chinese assumptions about dating and marriage?
3. According to your own cultural background, what are some assumptions about what makes a marriage work? Write two:
4. Basic cultural assumptions also define male and female character. They affect what we believe to be "natural" characteristics of males or "typical" female behavior. For example, an American cultural assumption about females is that they are emotional, in contrast to males, who are expected to be unemotional. Based on this assumption, most Americans learn early in life that "real" men don't cry, and they have trouble accepting a grown man in tears.

In your native culture, what characteristics are considered typical of males and females? For example, the dominant American culture considers females to be "emotional" and males to be "logical." In the spaces below, write five adjectives under MALE and five under FEMALE, based on the cultural assumptions of the society in which you grew up. Put a checkmark next to the ones that you also agree are true. When you have finished, pick two adjectives for each gender and write them on the board, while your classmates do the same. Discuss the similarities and differences in basic cultural assumptions about the male and female character.

IN MY NATIVE CULTURE

Males are supposed to be	Females are supposed to be	Agree?
1.	1.	
2.	2.	
3.	3.	
4.	4.	
5.	5.	

THINK ABOUT THIS

Can a male and female be "just friends"?

1. In your native culture, what do people think about this question?
2. Have you observed real friendships between males and females in the United States?
3. What do you think?

≡ With a Partner

1. Share your views on the questions above.
2. Together, make a list of some of the things that can make friendship between males and females difficult.
3. Get together with another pair and share your lists. Talk over some ways to get around these problems or obstacles.

Interviews and Analysis

 INTERVIEW TIP: COLLOQUIAL EXPRESSIONS
RELATED TO GENDER

There are many American expressions about issues related to being male and female that may not be in the dictionary. The following list may help you to understand your interview better and also life in the United States.

Battered wife — a wife who is beaten by her husband (illegal in the U.S.)

Blind date — a date between two people who do not know each other

Boyfriend — a male that a female is romantically involved with

To break up, to split up — to end a romantic relationship

To cheat (on) — when one partner in a relationship or marriage becomes sexually involved with someone else

Coeducational (coed) — male and female students together

Come-on (noun or verb) — something said just to interest someone sexually, often not true; very obvious flirting

A couple — two people who are either dating each other or are married

Day care — a place where babies and small children are taken care of while their parents are at work

Double date — a date on which two couples go out together

To flirt — verbal or nonverbal behavior meant to attract someone

Gay — interested in people of the same sex; a homosexual male

Girlfriend — a female friend (if said by another woman); a girl or woman that a man is involved with romantically (if said by a male)

To go out — to go on a date

To go together — to date just one person

To have an affair — to be involved in a sexual relationship with someone who is married

Macho — acting in an overly aggressive way, usually by a male, to prove his masculinity

To make out — to hug, kiss, and caress in a sexual way (slang)

Maternity leave, paternity leave — time off from work given to new parents, paid or unpaid

To pick (someone) up; (a pickup) — to introduce yourself to and leave with a stranger whom you find attractive

To turn (someone) on — to attract someone sexually

Sexist (sexism) — the idea of males being better than females; the idea of women as sex objects first and people second

Sexual harrassment — pressure from a boss or coworker, to change the relationship into a more sexual one

To sleep around — to have many lovers (slang)

Straight — interested in the opposite sex (slang)

Unwed mother — a woman who has a child without being married

The women's movement (women's lib) — an American social movement that began in the 1970's to fight for equal rights for women

☰ With a Partner of the Same Gender

Go over this list together. Make sure that you each understand the meanings of all the vocabulary words. Organize the list into groups that you think go together. Choose one group (five-word minimum) and together write a paragraph or story using all the words from that group.

Interview Instructions There are so many issues about males and females that this chapter divides the subject into three subtopics:

- What it Means to Be an American Male/Female
- Males and Females at Work in the U.S.
- American Romances

Decide which subtopic interests you the most by looking over the questionnaires beginning on page 147. After you decide, you will find out about your subtopic by getting together and forming a team with two classmates who are also interested in your subtopic. You will work together in a team, following these five steps to guide you in researching and presenting information about your subtopic.

☰ STEP 1: Teams Get Together

After you decide which questionnaire is most interesting to you, get together with two other classmates who chose the same one. If possible, your team should include both males and females and students from different cultural backgrounds.

Talk about why you are each interested in the topic. Based on this discussion, make up a team name. Together, think up one additional question related to your topic that you all want to find out about. Add it to your questionnaire.

☰ STEP 2: Interview Each Other

With your team, go over each question on the questionnaire, sharing how three of you would answer each one yourself. Also, talk about how most people from each of your native countries would answer the questions.

Make plans for the team to interview three American informants. Decide if you prefer to do group interviews or individual interviews, and whether teammates want to work together or by themselves.

☰ STEP 3: Interview American Informants

Use one of the following questionnaires. Warn your informant that the interview could take up to 30 minutes. Do not forget to ask your team's additional question and to write down any new vocabulary that you learn.

Questionnaire 1: Out-of-class

WHAT IT MEANS TO BE AN AMERICAN MALE/FEMALE

Ask an American informant to answer these questions.

Part I: To help us better understand male and female roles in the United States, how would you interpret the following situations? What you would think about the people involved in each one?

1. Your friend gives her four-year-old son a doll for his birthday.

_____

_____

2. A male friend meets a girl at a party, and she calls him up to ask him to go to the movies.

_____

_____

3. Your teenaged cousin complains that the boy she likes won't dance.

_____

_____

4. You hear a man say "Hey, baby" as a woman walks past him on the street.

_____

_____

5. You meet a woman at the library and she introduces you to her roommate, who is male.

_____

_____

6. The husband in a couple you know does all the cooking and laundry for the family.

_____

_____

7. You see a young man and a woman having a conversation. She is smiling a lot and looking him in the eye while they talk.

_____

_____

8. A woman you meet at a party tells you she is a feminist.

_____

_____

9. You see two women dancing together at a party.

_____

_____

10. You see your aunt's boss put his arm around her.

_____

_____

11. You see two girls holding hands in public.

_____

_____

12. While sitting in the park, you watch as a man picks up a woman and invites her for a drink. She accepts.

_____

_____

13. You see a young woman walking through the park late at night.

_____

_____

14. A male friend comes to talk over a problem he is having, and in the course of the conversation he begins to cry.

_____

_____

15. Your own question.

_____

_____

Part II:

1. What is the hardest part about growing up male in the United States?

_____

_____

2. What is the hardest part about growing up female here?

_____

_____

3. What are the most positive changes in American society in terms of what it means to be male and female here, or how males and females relate to each other?

_____

_____

Signature of informant: _____ Sex: _____ Age: _____

Race, religion, or ethnic group: _____

New vocabulary: _____

PAY, GENDER AND SCHOOLING
Median earnings of fulltime, year-round
American workers, age 25 and over, 1989

LESS THAN 4 YEARS OF HIGH SCHOOL	
$18,766	MEN
$11,919	WOMEN
4 YEARS OF HIGH SCHOOL	
$25,372	MEN
$16,108	WOMEN
SOME COLLEGE	
$29,256	MEN
$19,987	WOMEN
4 YEARS OR MORE OF COLLEGE	
$38,296	MEN
$25,929	WOMEN

SOURCE: US Census Bureau

....

THINK ABOUT THIS

Although it pays to get an education, in the United States it pays men more than women, according to the graph above. It shows the median pay for men and women at different educational levels, working full time in 1989. Median pay means that half the people make more, and half make less.

≡ With a Partner

1. Together, answer these questions about the chart above. Take turns doing the math, checking it, and circling the correct answer. **Who can expect to make more money:**

   Example: (a man) or a woman with some college experience

   a. a man or a woman with less than four years of high school?
   b. a man with less than four years of high school or a woman with four years of high school?
   c. a man with some college or a woman with four years or more of college?
   d. a man with four years of high school or a woman with four years of college?

2. For each of you, find the median pay for someone of your gender and same years of schooling.

3. Does the graph show that it makes sense financially for each of you to complete your education?

4. Based on this graph, could each of you expect to make more or less money if you were of the opposite gender (i.e. a man or a woman)?

5. Together, think about all the reasons that men make more money than women with the same educational qualifications. Choose two reasons that you think best explain why this is so. Write them down:

_____

_____

6. What do you think about what this graph shows? Write your opinions:

_____

_____

7. How does the situation shown in the graph compare with what men and women make in other countries? In what countries is the pay between men and women more equal?

_____

In what countries is the pay between men and women even less equal?

_____

≡ With Your Class

With your classmates, talk over the answers that you and your partner came up with for these questions.

Questionnaire 2: Out-of-class

MALES AND FEMALES AT WORK IN THE U.S.

Ask an American informant these questions:

1. What were the traditional careers or jobs for women in the United States? Why was that? How is it changing?

_____

_____

_____

2. What careers or positions had traditionally been filled by men? Why was that?
   How is it changing today?

   _____

   _____

   _____

   _____

3. Why do most of the women you know work?

   _____

4. According to statistics, the average American female worker does not earn nearly
   as much as the average American male worker. In your opinion, what are some of
   the reasons for this?

   _____

   _____

   _____

5. If a woman discovers that she is not paid as much as her male co-worker who does
   the same job, what usually happens? Are there any laws about this?

   _____

   _____

   _____

6. If a woman's boss pressures her to have sex with him, what usually happens? Are
   there any laws about this?

   _____

   _____

   _____

   _____

7. Why do you think more men than women are managers in the United States? Do you think this will change?

_____

_____

_____

8. Do most of the American women you know continue to work after they get married?   Why or why not?

_____

_____

_____

9. Do most of the women you know continue to work after they have children? Why or why not? Who provides the child care?

_____

_____

_____

10. Did the employers of the working mothers you know offer them any time off when they became mothers? Was it paid?

_____

11. Does the American government do anything to support families in which both parents work? Do American employers?

_____

_____

12. How do single mothers support their families?

_____

_____

13. What jobs have you held? Were males or females mostly in charge? In your opinion, have your male and female coworkers had the same opportunities? Would you say this is true for American society in general? Please explain.

_____

_____

14. Your own question.

_____

_____

Signature of American informant: _____ Sex: _____ Age: _____

Race, religion, or ethnic background: _____

New vocabulary: _____

....
THINK ABOUT THIS

Are little boys and little girls different — besides their physical differences?

1. Make a list of differences that you have observed between little boys and little girls.
2. Make a list of differences that you and most people you know agree are generally true.

≡ **With a Partner**

1. Combine your lists on the following chart:

LITTLE GIRLS	LITTLE BOYS

2. How do you explain the differences that you have observed? If you think that children are born with certain natural differences, write an "N" (for nature) next to it on the list. Write an "S" next to anything that you think is the result of the way that society (including the family) teaches males and females. If you and your partner do not agree about how to label some items, write both an "N" and an "S" next to them.

≡ **As a Class**

1. On one side of the board, your teacher will write "Nature" and on the other side he or she will write "Society." Go to the board and under "Nature," write down everything that you and your partner labelled "N." Then do the same on the other side of the board for the differences that you marked with an "S." Other pairs will do the same.

2. Look over the two columns. If some differences are written under both "Nature" and "Society," talk about them. Does the lack of agreement about what causes differences reflect either the genders or the cultural backgrounds of the classmates who disagree?

Questionnaire 3: Out-of-class

AMERICAN ROMANCE
Ask an American informant these questions:

1. Pretend you have just introduced two good friends, male and female, about your age. How can you tell if they are interested in each other? Be specific.

   _____

   _____

2. Afterward, you talk to each friend alone and find out that each found the other very attractive. What are some words that your male friend might use to describe your female friend? What are some words that your female friend might use to describe him?

   _____

3. What would probably happen next, if they did like each other?

_____

_____

4. If they began dating, describe a typical date they might go on:

_____

_____

5. If they went out together every weekend for a month, would you expect them to continue to date other people at the same time?

_____

6. How could you tell that your friends were getting serious? List some of the signs:

_____

_____

7. How would it affect things if your friends' parents were not happy about their relationship?

_____

_____

8. How would your friends' relationship be affected if they were from different religions? What about if they were from different ethnic backgrounds? Different races? Different classes?

_____

_____

_____

_____

_____

9. What would your reaction be if your friends told you that they were going to live together? What would their parents' reaction be?

_____

_____

10. What would you expect to happen if your female friend got pregnant?

_____

_____

11. Your friends seem to really love each other. How old do you think they should be to get married? Explain your reasons.

_____

_____

12. If they do get married, would you expect your female friend to keep her own name after marriage? Explain.

_____

13. Half of all American marriages end in divorce. Could you talk about some of the reasons?

_____

_____

14. Could you tell me some of the ways that AIDS has affected social life in the United States?

_____

_____

_____

_____

15. Your own question.

_____

_____

Signature of American informant: _____

Sex: _____ Age: _____ Race, religion, or ethnic background: _____

New vocabulary: _____

≡ STEP 4: Team Analysis and Planning

Once you have all interviewed American informants with your questionnaire, meet with your teammates to analyze your findings. Divide up these jobs: **discussion leader,** who will move things along and keep track of the time; **checker,** who will check to make sure that everyone in the group is participating; **praiser,** who will say something positive every time a teammate makes a contribution to the group.

Example: "That's a good point."

With your teammates, talk over how your interviews went. Discuss what you thought went well and what didn't go well. Then share the information that you each found out in the interview:

1. What did your informants say about each question?
2. What did they say that surprised you the most?
3. What were some similarities in how all the informants answered the questions? What were some differences?

After everyone on the team has reported about his or her interview, take a few minutes to write down your answers to this question:

From all the information that you and your teammates learned from interviewing an American informant, what do you think is most important for those learning English in the United States to know about?

After you have made a few notes, share your answers with your teammates and talk over your ideas. Using this information, plan a skit to present to the class that shows the most important things you learned in your interviews.

≡ STEP 5: Performance

Perform your team's skit for your other classmates. Afterward, ask your classmates how they understood the skit and how it fits in with their own experiences.

JOURNAL

Among people from your cultural background, what are some common stereotypes about American males and American females? List them like this:

STEREOTYPES	
AMERICAN MALES	AMERICAN FEMALES

Then write what you think about these stereotypes. Why do people believe them? How do you think people from different cultures can learn the truth about each other better? Finally, write about how the work that you and your classmates have done in this chapter has changed your ideas.

Additional Activities

ESSAY

Get together with someone from your native country. Choose one of the following topics and talk over how it is currently thought about and dealt with where you come from:
   women in government * sexual harrassment * day care * housework * unwed mothers
   Together, write an essay about your topic, following these steps:

1. Make notes on your conversation, and if necessary, brainstorm some additonal ideas and write them down. Think about the following questions: How have people's ideas about the issue changed? Do men and women disagree on the issue? What are the different "sides" to the issue? Has religion influenced how people feel?
2. Decide on one main idea for your essay and write it in one sentence. This will be your topic sentence.
3. Make an outline for an essay of two or more paragraphs. Work on this together.
4. Following the outline, choose one or more paragraphs to write on your own, while your partner writes another.
5. After you have each written your paragraphs, trade them and correct each other's draft. Talk over your corrections.
6. Decide who will copy over the final essay and who will read it to the class.

....
DEBATES

Get back together with your team. Find another team to debate one of the following issues and decide which team will defend which side of the issue.

1. Mothers with young children should stay home/should be able to work.
2. Women should/should not ask men out.
3. We need/do not need laws to protect homosexuals.
4. Colleges should/should not permit coed dormitories.
5. Couples should/should not live together before marriage.

   After choosing a side, each team will work together to prepare a list of arguments, or reasons, to support its position. The team will then chooses three members to speak during the debate. The first speaker will state the team's position and explain why the issue is important, the second speaker will present the team's arguments, and the third speaker will answer the other team's arguments, or points.

   Both teams will debate in front of the class. Using a scorecard (see below), the class will decide the winner. First, the teams flip a coin to see which one begins. Then, the first speaker from Team A has one minute (maximum) to state the team's position and explain why it is important. The first speaker from Team B then has one minute to do the same. Next, the second speaker from Team A presents Team A's arguments (four-minute maximum), followed by the presentation from the second speaker from Team B. The third speaker from Team A then has two minutes to answer Team B's arguments. Finally, Team B's third speaker responds to the arguments presented by Team A (two-minute maximum).

SCORECARD

Rate the speakers from each team on a scale of 1-5 (highest). Base your ratings on:

1. how clear was the presentation
2. how logical were the arguments
3. how factual (how many facts) was the case

Your ratings should NOT be based on your own opinions of the issue.

FIRST SPEAKER		SECOND SPEAKER		THIRD SPEAKER	
Team A	Team B	Team A	Team B	Team A	Team B

TOTAL POINTS Team A: _____
TOTAL POINTS Team B: _____

CHILDREN'S CARTOONS

One place American children learn what it is to be male and female in U.S. society is through television cartoons. Watch an American children's cartoon, such as Smurfs, GI Joe, or even Mickey Mouse. These can be rented in any video store, or they can be seen on Saturday morning television. Observe what the male and female characters are like, including animals. What do the male characters do? What do the female characters do? What do they look like? What do they sound like? What lessons do they learn? After you have watched a cartoon and taken notes on these questions, prepare a list of adjectives that describe:

Male characters:

_____

_____

Female characters:

_____

_____

Share your list of adjectives with the class and talk over how these might affect young children's development.

Chapter 8

Time

Warm-up

....
THINK ABOUT THIS

In English, people who prefer the night are known as "night owls," while morning people are known as "early birds." Other people feel their best at other times of day.
   What is your favorite time of the day (or night)? Why?

☰ Line Up

1. Stand up with your classmates and form a line. Place yourself in the line according to your favorite time of day. Find out who likes to get up the earliest and put that person at one end. Everyone else will find a place in line according to what time of day they feel their best.
2. Talk to the people on either side of you about how you feel at different times of day and how you would like to make your life fit your body's schedule.
3. Beginning with the earliest bird in the class, go down the line, saying your favorite time of day.
4. Leave the line and do a short interview with a classmate who chose a different time from you.

JOURNAL

Do you know anyone who is always late? Write about that person, giving examples. Then explain why you think he or she is always late, and how people who know that person, including yourself, feel about it.

Preparation

*Martha was an American student who was spending a summer in an Indonesian vil-
lage as part of a student exchange program. When she got the letter telling her that she
had been chosen to participate in the program, she felt very lucky. She was sure it was
going to be the most exciting experience of her life. She did not even feel a bit sad
about leaving behind her busy schedule back home: her part-time job at a fast-food
restaurant, the softball team, her volunteer work tutoring poor children, her evenings
out with friends, and her plans to take a summer school course.*

*The first few days after her arrival in Indonesia were filled with meeting her new
Indonesian family and their friends, trying new foods, walking around the village, and
getting to know her Indonesian exchange sister, Ketty. It was just as exciting as Martha
had hoped. But by her second week in the village, Martha began to feel that something
was wrong.*

*One morning after breakfast, she looked at her watch and asked Ketty, "So, what are
the plans for today? What are we going to do?"*

*Ketty replied, "Oh, I didn't really make any plans. My mother might want us to go
shopping with her later. Then we'll see what we feel like doing."*

Martha answered, "What time is your mom going shopping?"

*"Oh, whenever she's ready. Are you getting bored, Martha? Maybe we should take
you to the city. There is more going on there. The pace is faster, probably more what
you're used to. We could take a tour. I know the big hotels organize special tours of the
city for American tourists. Would you like that?"*

*"Oh, no, I don't want to be a tourist. I want to do just what you do. I guess I'm just
used to being busy all the time. It's hard for me to get used to not having plans. I feel
like I'm wasting my time if I don't have a full schedule," said Martha.*

"Don't you enjoy just relaxing in the summer?" asked Ketty.

*"No, I guess it makes me feel guilty. I'm happier when I'm busy. And besides, I'm only
here for two months. I don't want to leave Indonesia feeling that I haven't experienced
as much as I can. Let's go do something, Ketty." She looked down at her watch again
and exclaimed, "Goodness, it's almost 11 and all we've done is sat around talking!"*

*Ketty looked worried and said: "I feel bad for you, Martha. Maybe you would have
been happier with a family in the city," said Ketty.*

≡ **On Your Own**

Write the answers:

1. What are some words you would use to describe Martha's life back home?
2. What did Martha begin to feel was wrong?
3. How do Indonesians feel about time, according to the case study?
4. What do you think Martha meant about feeling "guilty"?

≡ **With a Partner**

1. Compare your answers to questions 1-4 above.
2. What do you think would make Martha's stay in Indonesia better for her? Talk over several possibilities, choose one you both agree on, and write it down.

....
THINK ABOUT THIS

What would a tourist visiting your country need to know about how people there deal with time?

≡ With a Partner from Your Cultural Background

1. Talk this over, brainstorming a list of customs and attitudes that visitors should know about. For example, when is it important to be on time and when is it expected that people arrive late? Do people make schedules for all their activities, including weekends or do they prefer to relax and let things happen?
2. List four of the most important customs or attitudes.
3. Find a pair from another background and take turns explaining your lists to each other.

....
BACKGROUND READING

In many ways, Martha's concept of time is typically American, or typically urban American. She worried about "wasting" her time in Indonesia if every minute was not planned. It was hard for her to be happy if she wasn't busy doing something. Many Americans also feel guilty if they aren't using time to get things done and accomplish their goals. In Martha's case, her goal was to experience everything she could in her summer in Indonesia. To her, experiencing Indonesia meant running around doing many things. She may have missed some important experiences of Indonesian life because she could not slow down and relax.

Anthropology, the study of different cultures, looks at how different cultural groups view time. Anthropologists try to understand whether people in a culture think of the past, the present, or the future, as most important. In many ways, the dominant culture in the United States is future-oriented. Americans will rush through the present in order to accomplish some future goal. Americans' desire for constant change is another example of their future orientation. Many Americans think that new is better than old, and that youth is the best time of life. Other cultures are more oriented toward the present or toward the past. For example, Ketty's idea of waiting until later to "see what we feel like doing" shows a present orientation. In Chinese culture, which is past-oriented, both tradition and old age are seen as more positive than they are by most members of the dominant American culture.

Anthropologists also try to understand cultural ideas about time by deciding if cultures are action-oriented or being-oriented. Although Martha's goal was to "experience" as much as she could in Indonesia, she didn't seem to think "sitting around" was an important experience. That is because most Americans value doing, or action, more than simply being. Why do so many Americans feel they must be busy to be happy? Perhaps the idea comes from the Puritans, the first English people to live in America. Their religion taught them about the "work ethic," the idea that work is morally good. The Puritans believed doing nothing was a sin. These ideas may help explain how uncomfortable, even guilty, many modern Americans like Ketty feel about activities that they see as "wasting time."

　　These are some of the differences in how people in different cultures think about time. However, there are also great differences within each country. For example, according to Ketty, city residents in Indonesia live a life that has a faster pace, more like the United States. On the other hand, in certain American regions such as the Southern states, California, and in small towns across the country, there is much less pressure about time than there is in the cities of the Northeast.

GLOSSARY FOR VOCABULARY USED IN CASE STUDY

Student exchange — programs in which students live in other countries, often with a family
Volunteer — without pay
Tutoring — teaching a small group or just one student, usually helping with schoolwork
Pace — speed; how fast things go
Urban — having to do with cities
Wasting — throwing away; not spending wisely
Accomplish — do, finish
Oriented (orientation) — interested in or focused on
Sin — against one's religion or against the will of God

☰ With a Partner from a Cultural Background Similar to Your Own

1. Talk over what is meant by past, present, and future orientation in the essay above. (You can use your native language.)
2. Write the examples for each that are given in the Background Reading.
3. Decide which orientation is most common in your native culture and circle:

    past　　　　present　　　　　future.

4. Write down two examples of customs, behaviors, or attitudes in your culture that show the time orientation you chose.
5. How do you both feel personally about the time orientation most common in your native culture? Talk it over.
6. Take turns saying one sentence for each glossary word above.
7. Talk over your plans to find an American informant to interview.

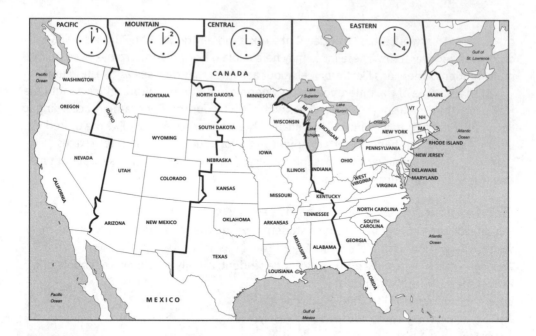

....
THINK ABOUT THIS

There are four time zones in the continental United States.

1. What time is it now in New York?
2. In Mississippi?
3. In New Mexico?
4. In Vermont?
5. In Delaware?
6. In Wyoming?
7. In Kansas?
8. In Oregon?

≡ With a Partner

1. Together, write down answers to these questions, taking turns this way: You find the answer to the first question and explain it to your partner, using the map. Your partner checks your answer and praises you if it is correct or helps you find a better answer if it is not. Then you switch roles and your partner tells you the answer to the next question, while you check the answer and praise or help out.
2. After you have done all eight, check your answers with another pair.
3. Meet alone with your partner again and write two more questions about what time it is in other states. For example: What time is it in Louisiana? Decide on the correct answer together.
4. Copy down your two questions and answers on a small piece of paper.

≡ Circle Quiz

1. Stand up with your book open to the map on page 168. Hold your paper with the two questions and answers you and your partner made up.
2. Form a circle with everyone in the class.
3. Go around the room, counting off "1, 2, 1, 2, etc." If you are a "1," stay where you are. If you are a "2," form an inside circle with the other "2"s, facing out to the circle of "1"s.
4. Facing your partner in the other circle, ask one of your questions. Praise your partner for a correct answer or help him or her find a better one. Then answer one of your partner's questions. Ask each other the other question.
5. When you have all finished quizzing each other, your teacher will tell you to rotate. The "1"s will stay in place, while the "2"s will move to their left by three people. When you have found your new partner, quiz each other just as you did before.
6. When you hear the signal, rotate again and quiz your new partner.

Interviews and Analysis

 INTERVIEW TIP: TIMING YOUR INTERVIEW

Because most Americans are so busy and aware of their time, it will help your informant if you talk about time limits when you are setting up the interview. When you ask someone if you can interview him or her, you should mention how much time the interview will take. For example, you might say, "The interview will not take more than a half hour." If you do this, you will not have to rush during the interview, because you and the informant will have reached an understanding about how long you will be together.

Setting up a time limit also means that you should time the interview. Look at your watch when you begin talking and figure out at what time you will finish asking the questions. Time the asking of the questions from the questionnaire according to this schedule, but do not rush. Remember, the best interviews are those during which your informant talks a lot. If your informant spends a lot of time on one question and you think that it is interesting information, you may decide that it is more important to listen, even if you do not get a chance to finish asking all your questions.

Once you have promised to end the interview at a certain time, you should keep your promise. If the informant seems interested in talking some more and you have the time, you might say, "I promised that we would end after a half hour. Do you need to go now? I'd be interested in talking some more if you're not in a rush." At the end, be sure to thank your informant by saying, "I really appreciate your time."

≡ Solve These Problems with Your Partner

What would you do in the following situations? Talk them over with your partner, and together think of the best way to respond. Write down what you would say in each situation. Then, get together with another pair and share your responses.

1. You finish asking all your questions in just ten minutes, but you haven't gotten many details.
2. Your informant spends 20 minutes answering the first question.
3. You've promised a half-hour interview, but you've forgotten your watch.

Questionnaire 1: In-class

CUSTOMS AND ATTITUDES ABOUT TIME

With your partner from the same (or similar) cultural background, talk over how most people would answer the following questions where you come from. Write down the answers that you and your partner agree are most typical.

1. In your culture, you invite friends for dinner and plan on eating at 9:00 P.M..
   a. At what time would you ask people to come? ___ : ___ (specific time)
   b. How would you feel if someone came at 10:00?

2. In your culture, you are invited to a dinner party for 9:00.
   a. At what time would you probably arrive? ___ : ___
   b. Why?

3. You are invited to a big dance in your native country that begins at 9:00.
   a. At what time would you probably arrive? ___ : ___
   b. Why?

4. In your native country, a friend has promised to meet you at a local coffee shop at 9:00, but he isn't there when you arrive.
   a. If he doesn't show up, at what time would you give up and leave? ___ : ___
   b. How would you feel about your friend being a half hour late?

5. You have promised to pick up your sister at 9:00 A.M. to go shopping, but you run into problems and arrive late.
   a. After what time would you feel like you had to say you were sorry for being late? ___ : ___
   b. What would you say?

6. You have a dentist's appointment for 9:00 A.M.

   a. At what time would you probably arrive? ___ : ___
   b. What would happen if you arrived late?
   c. In your native country, do dentists schedule appointments for specific times, the way they do in the United States?

7. You have a job interview at 9:00 A.M. in your native country.

   a. At what time would you probably arrive? ___ : ___
   b. What would happen if you arrived late?

8. What are three words in your native language that are used to describe someone who is always late? Translate them:

9. Are there words in your native language to describe someone who will do anything to avoid being late? Are they more positive or negative than the words in question 8?

10. Are your answers typical of the way most people from your culture would respond? If not, explain.

11. Would your answers to these questions have been different before coming to the United States? Explain.

12. In your culture, what time of life do people think is the best: childhood, youth, middle age, or old age? Why?

13. In your culture, what time of life do people think is the worst? Why?

Signature of partner: _____

Place of birth: _____

☰ With Your Partner

1. Go along with your partner on his or her interview with an American informant and help out by being the recorder, writing down the answers given by the informant.
2. Invite your partner to help you out in the same way during your interview with an American informant.

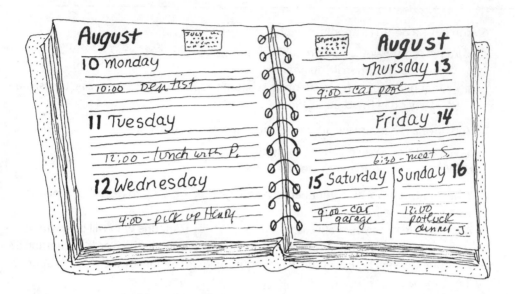

THINK ABOUT THIS

Many Americans do not like to make plans without first checking their schedule on their own calendar, also known as a datebook, an appointment book, or sometimes just "my book." These are used by many busy Americans to organize their work, school, and social lives.

1. Are datebooks common where you come from? Why or why not?
2. Why do you think so many Americans use them?

☰ With a Partner from Another Cultural Background

1. Share your answers to the questions above.
2. Get together with another pair and report on what your partner said. Listen to the reports of the other three students.

☰ Take Sides

1. If you use a calendar or datebook to remember your appointments, stand up and go to one side of the room with your other classmates who do; if you don't use one, go to the other side of the room where those who do not are standing.
2. Talk over the reasons why you do or do not use a datebook with one or two classmates on your side of the room.
3. Go over to the other side of the room and find out two reasons why someone there does or does not use a datebook. Write them down.
4. Together, talk about whether your ideas have changed since coming to the United States.

Questionnaire 2: Out-of-class

AMERICAN CUSTOMS AND ATTITUDES ABOUT TIME

Interview an American informant about attitudes regarding time in the United States. Make up one question of your own at the end. Write down any new vocabulary that you hear or learn.

1. Say you invite friends over for dinner and plan on eating at 9:00.

   a. At what time would you tell people to come? __ : __ (specific time)

   b. How would you feel if someone came at 10:00?

   _____

2. You are invited to a dinner party for 9:00.

   a. At what time do you usually arrive? __ : __

   b. Why?

   _____

3. You are invited to a big dance beginning at 9:00.

   a. At what time would you probably arrive? __ : __

   b. Why?

   _____

4. Say a friend has promised to meet you at a local coffee shop at 9:00, but he isn't there when you arrive.

   a. If he doesn't show up, at what time would you give up and leave? __ : __

   b. How would you feel about your friend being a half hour late?

   _____

5. You have promised to pick up your sister at her house 9:00 A.M. to go shopping, but you run into problems and arrive late.

   a. After what time would you feel like you had to say you were sorry for being late? __ : __

   b. What would you say?

   _____

6. You have a dentist's appointment for 9:00 A.M.

    a. At what time do you generally arrive?___:___

    b. What would happen if you arrived late?

    _____

7. You have a job interview at 9:00 A.M.

    a. At what time would you probably arrive?___:___

    b. What would happen if you arrived late?

    _____

8. What are the first three words that come to mind to describe someone who is always late?

    _____

9. What words would you pick to describe someone who will do anything to avoid being late?

    _____

10. Do you think that your answers to these questions are typical of the way most Americans might answer? Explain.

    _____

    _____

    _____

11. Are there any parts of the country that seem to have a different attitude about time? Explain.

    _____

    _____

12. What time of life do Americans think is the best: childhood, youth, middle age, or old age? Why?

_____

13. What time of life do Americans think is the worst? Why?

_____

14. Your own question.

_____

_____

_____

American informant interviewed: _____ Sex: _____

Place of birth: _____ Age: _____ Ethnic background: _____

Student? _____ Parents' jobs (if student): _____

Job: _____

New vocabulary: _____

ANALYSIS WITH YOUR PARTNER

1. Talk over how you each think your partner's interview went. Then talk about how you think your interview went. Discuss any problems and how you might do better the next time.
2. Compare the times given in answer to questions 1a through 7a on Questionnaire 1 (which you did together) and on Questionnaire 2 (which you each did with a different

American informant). Fill in the bar graph below to represent your data. First, help your partner fill in his or her bar graph, then work together on your own.

	11:00								
	10:30								
	10:00								
	9:30								
	9:00								
	8:30								

Informant from:	Informant from:	Informant from:	Informant from:
_____ U.S. (culture)	_____ U.S. (culture)	_____ U.S. (culture)	_____ U.S. (culture)
Question 1	Question 2	Question 3	Question 4
(dinner party)	(dinner party)	(dance)	(café)

	11:00					
	10:30					
	10:00					
	9:30					
	9:00					
	8:30					

Informant from:	Informant from:	Informant from:	
_____ U.S. (culture)	_____ U.S. (culture)	_____ U.S. (culture)	
Question 5	Question 6	Question 7	
(shopping)	(dentist)	(interview)	

3. Look over your bar graph and identify those questions in which the two bars look even, or almost the same height. Compare your observation with your partner's.
4. Look over your bar graph and identify those questions in which one bar is a lot taller than the other. Compare your observation with your partner's.
5. Based on your answers to the last two questions, would you say that there were more differences or similarities between the way people from the United States and people from your native country think about time?

ANALYSIS IN SMALL GROUPS

Form groups of four by getting together with another pair. Choose someone to fill these jobs: **calculator** (someone to do the math), **checker** (someone to check the math), **secretary** (someone to write the answers), and **reporter** (someone to tell the answers to the class).

1. Compare the questions and answers of everyone in the group to number 14, your own question on Questionnaire 2. As a group, decide which answer is the most important for those learning about American culture to know about, and write it down.

2. Share your bar graphs and talk about ways in which the American answers were similar to the answers in Questionnaire 1 and the ways in which they were different. Listen to what others in the group learned from their bar graphs. As a group, decide:

   a. which culture represented in the group has more similar answers to the American ones

   b. which culture has more different answers

3. Talk over any answers or explanations from American informants that you and your group did not understand. If after talking them over the group still does not understand some American responses, write them down, along with the group's questions.

4. In your group, compare the times given by American informants for questions 1a through 7a. Have the calculator figure out the average time for each question. (Do the math by adding up the times given for each question and dividing by the number of informants.) After these figures are checked by the checker, graph the average American times for each question, using the bar graph below:

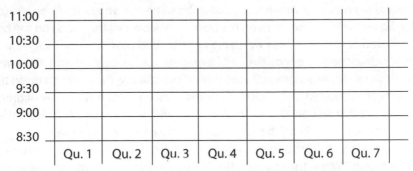

5. Identify the questions to which the average American response was 9:00. Identify the questions to which the average American response was *not* 9:00. Based on this data, write a statement on a separate piece of paper about the situations in which Americans think it is most important to be on time. Then write a statement about the situations in which Americans are more flexible about time.

   a. For Americans, it is most important to be on time in these situations:

   b. Americans are more flexible about being on time in these situations:

....
ANALYSIS IN CLASS

Note: The calculators should meet and figure out the average American times given in response to questions 1a through 7a, Questionnaire 2. The calculators will use the averages that the small groups have already calculated to answer question 4 on page 177. After the calculators have figured out the averages for the class, the checkers should fill out a bar graph (using as a model the small-group bar graphs) on the board or overhead projector. This bar graph will show the times given by all the American informants interviewed by the class in response to questions 1a through 7a.

   Meanwhile, the reporters from each small group will share answers to these questions with the class, based on information written down by the secretaries in each group:

1. What was the most important information each group learned from the questions students made up to ask American informants (answer to Analysis in Small Groups question 1)?
2. Which culture did each small group find was most similar to the United States in their customs and attitudes toward time (answer to Analysis in Small Groups question 2)? Which culture was the most different?
3. Were there any unclear answers or explanations given by American informants that need to be made clearer?

Questions for General Class Discussion
4. What words were used by Americans to describe someone who is always late (Questionnaire 2, question 8)? Someone will write these on the board. Discuss any terms that are not clear.
5. What words were used by Americans to describe someone who hates to be late (question 9)? Someone will write these on the board. Look over all the words on the board. As a class, decide which of these words are negative and have someone circle them. Decide which are neutral or positive and have someone underline them. Talk over what the words say about American attitudes toward punctuality, the ability to be on time.
6. What parts of the United States did Americans think had a different view of time (Questionnaire 2, question 11)? Go to the board and write down what your informant said. Your classmates will do the same. Locate these regions on a map.
7. What time of life was most popular among Americans? Does this indicate future or past orientation? When the checkers finish their bar graph, summarizing the whole class' interview data from Questionnaire 2, take some time to look it over together. Find out if anyone interviewed had very different responses and discuss their explanations. Can these differences be explained by age, background, or other factors?
8. Read the statements written in small groups about the situations in which Americans feel it is most important to be on time, and those situations in which time is more flexible (Analysis in Small Groups question 5). According to the information from the whole class, summarized in the bar graph, which of these statements is true?

JOURNAL
To complete Questionnaire 1, you had to give some thought to the attitudes toward time in your own culture. Did you learn anything new from this, including your discussions with your partner? Explain.

Additional Activity

PROVERBS RESEARCH

Using books on proverbs in the library, find some international proverbs that have to do with time. Write each one down, name the country of origin, and state your ideas about what the proverb tells us about that culture's attitudes toward time. For example, the Irish saying "The older the fiddle [violin], the sweeter the tune" teaches that getting older has some advantages. Draw lines between proverbs from different cultures that seem to say the same thing in different words or images.

Chapter 9

Money

Warm-up

....
THINK ABOUT THIS

You have just met someone at a party, and you admire her watch. Would you ask how much the watch cost?

≡ Take Sides

1. Stand up and go to one side of the room with your classmates who answered the question the same way that you did (yes or no).
2. Pair up and talk about why you feel the way you do.
3. Observe who is standing on each side. Are students from certain cultural backgrounds more likely to be on one side of the room?
4. Share the reasons from each side of the room.

JOURNAL

Many people learn about Americans from watching American movies, where most of the people shown are upper middle class. Are the actual Americans whom you have met or seen in the United States richer or poorer than you thought they would be? Give some examples. How do you fit in? Do you feel richer or poorer in the United States than you do in your native country? How do you feel about that?

Preparation

CASE STUDY

José and Jim were neighbors. They had become friendly because both of them were also studying at the same university. Jim was studying business, and José planned to be an engineer, but he was taking English classes first.

One day they ran into each other as they were leaving their apartment building. Jim asked José, "José, I need a favor. Can you spare a dollar? I have to go over to school, and I'm flat broke. If you lend me a buck, I'll be able to take the bus. I can pay you back tomorrow."

"Sure, Jim. No problem. You don't have to pay me back," said José, as he handed Jim a dollar.

As soon as he got home the next day, Jim went over to José's to return the dollar. When José opened his door, Jim said, "Here's your dollar, man. It sure came in handy — I would have frozen if I'd had to walk."

"Forget it," said José, as he handed back Jim's dollar.

"Oh, no, I insist. I couldn't take advantage of you. What if I needed to borrow money again sometime? If I didn't pay you back now, I could never come back for more," said Jim, as he stuffed the dollar into José's shirt pocket.

José answered, "But that's what friends are for. In Spanish, we have a saying: 'Today for you, tomorrow for me.' If you pay me back, I will feel that I won't be able to ask you for money when I need it. I'll feel like you are closing the door on me, that there is no trust between us. I thought we were friends. How can I take the money?" José handed back the dollar.

"But I won't feel right if you don't take it," said Jim.

GLOSSARY FOR VOCABULARY USED IN CASE STUDY

To run into — to meet accidentally, without planning to (idiom)

Favor — the act of doing something nice for someone else, helping someone out

To spare — to do without, to let go of

Flat broke/broke — (completely) out of money (slang)

To lend — to give something with an understanding that it will be returned

Buck — a dollar (slang)

To come in handy — to be very useful; to come at a good time (idiom)

To insist — to continue to ask; to refuse to take no for an answer

To stuff — to shove; to fill something in a hurry

To take advantage of — to exploit; to abuse; to make someone into a victim

Trust — mutual understanding, the feeling that you can depend on another person

. . . .
THINK ABOUT THIS

1. If you were Jim, would you return the dollar?
2. If you were José, would you accept the dollar?
3. Are your answers typical of your cultural background?
4. What values do you think your answers reflect?

≡ With a Partner

Talk over the questions above, explaining your answers to each other. Together, take turns writing down the answers to these questions.

5. Why did Jim want to return the dollar to José?
6. Why did José not accept the dollar?
7. What do you think will happen between José and Jim?
8. Take turns writing a sentence each for every vocabulary word in the glossary.

··················

THINK ABOUT THIS

In most restaurants in the U.S., customers tip between 15% and 20% of the final bill for the meal.

1. In what restaurants do customers *not* have to tip at all?
2. What are some situations in which you should not tip 15%?

≡ With a Partner

1. Compare your answers to these questions and choose an answer for each that you both agree on. Write them below:

_____

_____

2. Be ready to share your answer with the rest of the class.
3. Talk over whether the customs about restaurant tipping are different in your native countries.

······················
BACKGROUND READING

One reason that José did not want to accept Jim's dollar was because in Latin-American cultures, as in many others, it is very important to be generous. José lent Jim the dollar because generosity is an important value in his culture. When Jim insisted on paying back the dollar, José saw this as questioning or insulting his generosity. This made José question whether he and Jim were really friends.

In Arab, Latin, Greek, and Italian cultures, where generosity is such an important value, being stingy is a terrible way to be, and calling someone else cheap is a serious insult. Carmen Judith Nine Curt, who has written on this cultural issue, explains that to return a small amount of money in Caribbean culture suggests that the person who lent the money is stingy. José was insulted that Jim seemed to think that he was so stingy that he needed his dollar back.

Many Americans see it all differently. Jim felt that it would be rude if he did *not* try to return the dollar as soon as possible. To understand the dominant American point of view, it is neces-sary to know how important it is for Americans to think of themselves as independent when it comes to money. Americans do not mind owing money to banks, but many Americans feel very uncomfortable if they owe money or favors to friends or family. In American culture, owing too many favors means being dependent, which Americans see as a weakness. They do not like to think of themselves as "sponges" or "mooches," negative words in American slang that are used to describe people who take too much from other people.

Traditionally, Americans prefer to be "free" of obligations, debts, and favors. They feel strongly about paying their own way. To let someone else pay for them is seen as taking advantage of others, and this is morally wrong. Only if Jim and José were very close friends would Jim feel that he was not taking advantage of José by not paying back the dollar.

The case study is an example of two culturally different attitudes toward money. But it also shows something about two culturally different ideas about friendship. To José, giving Jim money when he needed it was a way to build their friendship. José expected that instead of paying back the dollar, Jim would later do a favor for José, and José would then do Jim another favor, and so on. Friendship in Latin culture is based on the values of inter-dependence and mutual obligation, much like the relations in Latin family life. Most Americans, on the other hand, feel that too much dependence on another person, especial-ly financial dependence, can hurt a friendship. Many Americans are careful not to let money come between friends.

GLOSSARY FOR BACKGROUND READING VOCABULARY
Insult — to question in a negative way
Generous (generosity) — free in giving (of money, favors, or time); happy to share
Stingy — not generous; selfish with money; cheap
Weakness — lack of strength
Debt — something owed to someone else; an amount of money that someone has bor-rowed and must return
Mutual obligation — a system in which people do favors for each other, where people feel they owe something to each other

ON YOUR OWN

1. Write two examples of others' generosity that you have observed.
2. Write two examples of financial independence in your own life.

≡ With a Partner

Take turns making up oral sentences for each vocabulary word glossed in the Background Reading.

≡ In a Group of Three

Look over the advertisements and coupons on page 186 and together answer:

1. Where would you purchase the products advertised on page 186?
2. Are any of these offers good today?
3. At which store would you save the most?
4. Which one is not a coupon?
5. What else do you have to do besides buy ginger ale to get the value of that coupon?
6. What do they wash at Rub n' Scrub?
7. Is the free Maxi Burger coupon valid at any David's?
8. To get your money back, do you turn in all of the coupons on this page at the stores?
9. For which of the coupons on this page will get you cash back?
10. What are double coupons?
11. Have you used any coupons yourself since coming to the United States?
12. Do you have coupons in your native country?

Answers:

1. Rub n' Scrub; at any drugstore; Oscar's clothing store; David's; Shopper's World grocery store. 2. Yes. 3. Oscar's. 4.Oscar's. 5. Buy $5 in groceries. 6. Cars. 7. No. 8. No. 9. Hold-It Hairspray cash refund. 10. When stores offer to pay double the value of each coupon.

Interviews and Analysis

 INTERVIEW TIP: SLANG EXPRESSIONS ABOUT MONEY

Money seems to be an area in which there are many slang expressions. When you interview an American informant, you may hear some of the following idioms or slang:

To go Dutch, to split the tab — idioms meaning that everyone pays their own way (for example at a restaurant or a movie theater)

Treat — a noun or a verb indicating that one person will pay for another, as in "The movie is my treat" or "Let me treat you to dinner."

Cheapskate — slang for a stingy person

To haggle, to bargain someone down — to try to get a better price (not slang)

Dough, bread — slang expressions for cash ("bucks" means dollars, as in "Lend me three bucks.")
Loaded — slang for rich, wealthy
To rip (someone) off — to steal from someone or to cheat someone
Bargain — a standard English noun meaning to buy something at good price, as in "The dress was a bargain at $30."

≡ **With a Partner**
Write a dialogue about two friends going shopping, in which you use five of the terms above.

Interviews and Analysis

Questionnaire 1: In-class

MONEY QUESTIONS
You have probably seen lottery tickets for sale in many small stores in the United States. Many people buy them because if you choose the right number, you can get rich. Many others never buy lottery tickets. Find a partner in the class who feels the same way that you do about buying lottery tickets. Interview each other about the following questions.

1. Imagine this situation: You suggest to a friend of the same sex, "Let's go out for lunch." When the check comes for the meal, who pays? Why? Is that the usual custom in your culture?
2. Imagine this situation: You go out on a date to the movies with someone of the opposite sex. Who would you expect to pay for the evening? Why? Is that the usual custom in your culture?
3. Imagine this: You borrow a quarter from a friend to make a phone call. The next time you see your friend, do you return the money? Why or why not? Would your friend accept it? Why or why not?
4. Imagine this: You need $25 for an emergency. To whom would you go to borrow the money? Would you return it? What would happen if you did not pay it back?
5. Imagine this: The college that you want to attend costs $2,000 more than you have. Where, or from whom, would you try to borrow the money? In your native country, when people are in this situation, what choices do they have?

6. Imagine this situation: The semester is ending, and you want to thank your favorite teacher for all her help. Would you buy her a pretty bracelet for $20 (if you had the money) to thank her? Why or why not? What would she think if you did?
7. Imagine this situation: You are returning to your native country. While waiting at customs, you notice that the customs official is giving people a hard time at the front of the line. Do you try to give the official some money when it is your turn, to avoid problems? Why or why not? In your native country, do people tip government employees in order to get a job done well or quickly?
8. In your culture, is it OK to ask friends how much money they make? Why or why not?
9. Is it OK to ask friends what they paid for their car? Their house? If not, why not?
10. Do you think it is OK to ask these questions of someone you have just met, or an acquaintance? Explain.
11. How would you feel if a guest at your house asked you how much you paid for your stereo?

Signature of partner: _____ Native culture: _____

≡ With Your Partner

1. Compare the ways in which each of you answered the questions above. Fill in the Venn diagram by writing the numbers of the questions that you answered the same way in the space in the middle where the circles overlap.

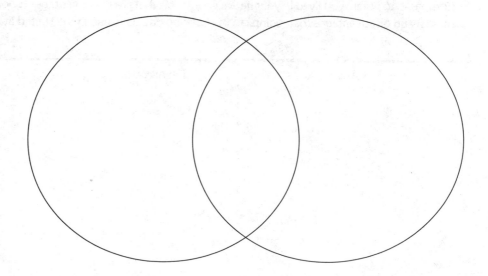

2. Choose two of the questions that you answered differently and think of a situation for each that could cause a misunderstanding. Write them down.

3. Talk over your plans to interview an American informant for Questionnaire 2.

APT. AVAIL. NOW!
Sunny furn. 2BR, mod K & B, lvg. rm.
w/ frpl. Pkg. $750 + util. No fee.

· · · · · · · · · · · · · · · ·
DID YOU KNOW?

When renting an apartment, you are usually required to pay the landlord an amount total-ing two months' rent before moving in. The first half counts as your first month's rent, and the second half is left as a "security deposit" until you move out. If you leave the apartment in good condition, your landlord should accept your security deposit as your last month's rent, or return the money to you if you pay the last rent. Sometimes you may also be required to pay a broker's fee to the real estate company that shows you the apartment. This fee, often half the amount of a month's rent, is not returned.

≡ **With a Partner**

Take turns writing down these answers:

1. How much money must be paid to the landlord before moving into the apartment advertised here?

2. How much must be paid to the real estate broker?

3. What rooms does this apartment have?

4. Describe your ideal apartment.

5. Compared to where you lived in your native countries, what are the advantages (good points) and disadvantages (bad points) to the housing you have had in the United States:

ADVANTAGES	DISADVANTAGES

Questionnaire 2: Out-of-class

MONEY QUESTIONS

Interview an American with the following questions, including a question of your own, at the end. Write down any new vocabulary you hear or learn in the course of the interview.

1. Imagine this situation: You suggest to a classmate of the same sex, "Let's go out for lunch after class." When the check comes for the meal, who pays? Why? Is that typical in the U.S.?

   _____

   _____

2. Imagine this situation: You go out on a date to the movies with someone of the opposite sex. Who would you expect to pay for the evening? Why? Is that typical?

   _____

   _____

   _____

3. Imagine this: You borrow a quarter from a friend to make a phone call. The next time you see your friend, do you return the money? Why or why not? Would your friend accept it? Why or why not?

   _____

   _____

4. Imagine this: You need $25 for an emergency. To whom would you go to borrow the money? Would you return it? What would happen if you did not pay it back?

   _____

   _____

   _____

   _____

5. Imagine this: The college that you want to attend costs $2,000 more than you have. Where, or from whom, would you try to borrow the money?

_____

_____

_____

_____

6. Imagine this situation: The semester is ending, and you want to thank your favorite teacher for all her help. Would you buy her a a pretty bracelet for $20? Why or why not? What would she think if you did?

_____

_____

_____

_____

7. Imagine this situation: While waiting at customs, you notice that the customs official is giving people a hard time at the front of the line. Do you slip the official some money when it is your turn, to avoid hassles? Why or why not? In the United States, do people tip government employees in order to get a job done well or quickly?

_____

_____

_____

_____

8. In the U.S., is it OK to ask friends how much money they make? Why or why not?

_____

_____

_____

9. Is it OK to ask friends what they paid for their car? Their house? If not, why not?

_____

_____

_____

10. Is it OK to ask these questions of someone you have just met, or an acquaintance? Explain.

_____

_____

_____

11. How would you feel if a guest at your house asked you how much you had paid for your stereo?

_____

_____

12. Your own question.

_____

_____

_____

_____

Signature of American informant: _____ Sex: _____

Place of birth: _____ Age: _____ Ethnic background: _____

Student? _____ Work (or parents' work): _____

New vocabulary: _____

≡ Pair Work

Work with your partner from Questionnaire 1 if you are from different countries. If you are from the same country, invite another pair from another country/countries to join you. Together, fill out the charts below about tipping and bargaining customs in your native countries. Then look at the American customs that are filled in and talk about any that you have observed. Together, write one question about an American tipping or bargaining custom that you would like to find out about:

How Much to Tip?

Fill in how much you would tip in the following situations back in your native countries. Write "N/A" if tipping is not appropriate.

	in _____:	in _____:	in U.S.:
Taxi driver			15%
Bartender			Change
Porter (hotel or airport)			$1/ bag
Bus driver			N/A
Hotel maid			Optional
Hairdresser or barber			15%
Servant in home in which you are a guest			N/A
Gas station attendant			N/A
Tour guide			$1
Washroom attendant			loose change
Coatroom attendant			Posted fee or $1

Together, write a question about U.S. tipping customs:

_____

_____

_____

WHEN TO BARGAIN?

Indicate the places in which you would try to bargain for a better price back in your native country, writing "A" for *always,* "S" for *sometimes,* and "N" for *never:*

	in _____:	in _____:	in U.S.:
Clothing store			N
Street vendor			S
Food store			N
Bookstore			N
Outside farmer's market			S
Yard sale/ Moving sale			S
Apartment rental			S
Taxi ride			N
House purchase			A
New car			A
Used car			A
Electronics Store			S

ANALYSIS IN GROUPS OF FOUR

With your partner from Questionnaire 1, form a group of four by finding another pair. Choose a **discussion leader,** a **timekeeper,** a **secretary,** and a **reporter.** The discussion leader will ask the group the following questions and the recorder will write down the answers to every question followed by an asterisk (*). The reporter will tell the whole class how the group answered these. Share your answers to the following questions in the group:

1. Who were your American informants? Without telling names, talk about who each of you interviewed.

2. How did the interview go? Were there any problems that the group could help with for the next time?
3. What questions did everyone ask on their own (question 12)? What answers did you get?
4. Choose the most interesting answer to question 12 from among all those collected by the group.*
5. What answers did everyone in the group get for questions 1 through 7? Find out each group member's answer before moving on to the next question.
6. Write down the question or questions to which American informants gave more different answers (from each other), and what those answers were.*
7. What answers did everyone get for questions 8 through 11?
8. Compare these answers to the customs in your own native countries. Discuss any embarrassing conversations that you know of that may have resulted from these cultural differences.
9. Choose an answer to question 6 or question 8 as the basic idea for a skit. Plan and practice a skit or role-play that shows a misunderstanding about money between people from the same or different cultures.

ANALYSIS IN CLASS

1. On the board, write down the question about U.S. tipping customs that you and your partner thought up. The other pairs in the class will do the same. Discuss your answers in class.
2. The reporter from each group of four will tell the class about the most interesting answer the group collected to question 12 in questionnaire.
3. The reporters will share with the class each group's analysis of question 6 (Analysis in Small Groups), the different answers given by American respondents to the same question. Discuss each of the explanations given.
4. Perform for the class the skit that you planned in your group of four.

JOURNAL

What has been the most confusing thing for you about dealing with money in the United States? Write about what it was like for you getting used to, for example, the change in currency.

606

62-19402617

PAY TO THE ORDER OF _City University_ ____ September 10 19 93

$ 20 00/00

Twenty dollars and 00/00 ____ DOLLARS

FIRST HERITAGE BANK

MEMO ____ _Helen Woolf_ ____

⑆3ᒪ7ᴏᴏᴊᴏ⑆ 9ᴏ27ᴏ926ᴏ 2ᴵᴵ 3ᴏ72

....
THINK ABOUT THIS

In order to accept a personal check, most businesses in the United States ask you for a major credit card and a form of identification with a photo, such as a license or passport.

1. What else might a business ask for before accepting her/his check?
2. What is an advantage of using traveler's checks? Where can you obtain these?

≡ With a Partner

1. Compare your answers to the questions above. Be ready to share them with the class.
2. Tell each other about your own experiences using checks in the United States.

....
THINK ABOUT THIS

Credit card companies make money from the interest paid by people who do not pay their monthly bills on time. Even though the bill tells you the minimum amount you must pay, the credit card company usually charges a finance charge of up to 20% (yearly rate) of whatever you do not pay when your bill is due.

1. Do you have a credit card? Why or why not?
2. Do you think more males or females tend to hold credit cards?
3. Do you think cardholders tend to have lived in the United States longer than those who do not hold credit cards?

☰ Take Sides

1. If you have a credit card, go to the side of the room where other cardholders are standing. If you do not have one, go to the other side. Talk over your reasons for having or not having credit cards.
2. Before you return to your seat, look at the people on each side and notice:
   • which side has more females?
   • on which side are there more students who have been in the U.S. longer?

   Raise your hand if one of your guesses was correct. Raise two hands if both guesses were correct.
3. Together with your classmates, fill in this bar graph:

SOME CHARACTERISTICS OF CREDIT CARD HOLDERS

25						
20						
10						
5						
0						
	non-cardholders	cardholders	cardholders	cardholders	cardholders	cardholders
	TOTAL		FEMALE	MALE	less than 1 year in U.S.	1 yr. + in U.S.

Additional Activities

....
LETTER OF ADVICE

Imagine that your cousin is moving to the United States. Write him or her a letter of advice on adjusting to American customs and attitudes regarding money. Advise your cousin about what to do and what not to do.

SYMBOLISM ON U.S. CURRENCY

Get together with your small group of four again. You will be assigned to find out about the symbols and writing that appear on one piece of U.S. money: Look at the animals, the buildings, the words, etc. Each group will be assigned to find out about a different denomination, such as a five-dollar bill or a quarter.

In your group, prepare a presentation for the rest of the class that includes some sort of visual display. Take turns so that everyone in the group reports on some aspect of the money that you found out about. Each group member should include a visual display in their presentation. Take notes so that at the end of all the reports, you will be able to say one piece of information about each denomination that was explained.

Chapter 10

Eating

Warm-up

Americans like hotdogs. This is a *generalization* that is mostly true, but there are also vegetarians in the United States. Vegetarians do not like meat. This statement is another generalization.

1. What have you learned about what Americans like to eat?
2. Write down three generalizations about what or how Americans like to eat.

≡ Stand Up for What You Think

1. Go to the board and write down two of your generalizations. Your classmates will do the same. Go back to your seat.
2. Someone will read each generalization out loud. After each generalization is read out loud, stand up if you think it is mostly true.
3. If there is anyone in the class who is sitting down, the reader will put a question mark next to that generalization.
4. Sit down. Repeat for each generalization.
5. After all the generalizations have been read, discuss the ones marked with a question mark. Copy down the generalizations and write a question mark next to those that you are not sure are mostly true. Save this paper for later in the chapter.
6. Someone will read the generalizations again. This time stand up after each one that is true for what or how *you* like to eat.

JOURNAL
What do you miss most about the food back home? Write about a favorite meal or dish, describing the ingredients, taste, and what your personal associations with it are (for example, when did you eat it, with whom, who cooked it, etc.).

Preparation

At the end of her first semester in an American college, Elsa, an student from Greece, was surprised to hear her chemistry professor invite the whole class to a party at his house.

"I hope y'all can come to the barbecue," he announced in a Southern accent. "I'll throw some hamburgers and dogs on the grill, but the rest is potluck. I hope we have some good cooks in the class!"

Elsa was happy to have the chance to try some American home cooking, after eating in the college cafeteria all semester. She did not want to generalize about American food based on just what was served in the cafeteria — it was pretty bad. She wanted to see what real American food was like.

After Elsa found out that "potluck" meant that the guests would each bring some food themselves, she decided to prepare a traditional Greek dish called spanakopitta, *a spinach pie. The problem was she did not have a kitchen.*

The next day in class, she said to Jeanette, an American classmate who often sat next to her, "Since I live in the dorm, it will be hard for me to cook anything for the barbecue. Where are you cooking?"

"Oh, I have an apartment off-campus with my boyfriend. Why don't you cook in my kitchen?"

The morning of the barbecue, Elsa went over to Jeanette's and found her preparing a salad out of grains, parsley, and tomatoes. Jeanette explained it was called tabbouleh.

"But I used to eat a salad just like that in Greece!" laughed Elsa when she saw Jeanette pouring on the olive oil. "Is that a typical American dish?"

"No, it's Middle Eastern. But my grandmother is from Lebanon, and it's always been my favorite salad. And now it's quite popular. I even saw it one day in the caf at school," said Jeanette.

Just then Rick, Jeanette's boyfriend, walked into the kitchen with three bags of potato chips. "I wanted to make sure that there would be something at the party for me to eat," he said.

"My junk food junkie," smiled Jeanette, as she patted him on the arm.

"Yeah, and Jeanette's a health food nut!" answered Rick.

Jeanette smiled, but she was still confused. She was not sure that she had become any clearer about American eating habits or what real American food was really like. She hoped she would find out at the party.

GLOSSARY FOR VOCABULARY USED IN CASE STUDY

Y'all — a slang expression used in the American South that means the plural of "you"; a short, slang form of the standard form "you all"

Barbecue — an outdoor social event at which people eat food that has been cooked on an open fire

Dogs — slang for "hot dogs" (Eating real dogs is taboo in the United States.)

Potluck — a type of social event to which each guest brings something to eat or drink

Dorm — abbreviation for dormitory (slang)

Off-campus — Property near a college or university that is not owned by the college; literally, off of the university campus

Caf — abbreviation for cafeteria (slang)

Junk food — food that is not very good for you, usually containing a lot of sugar, salt, or fat

Junkie — an addict; originally someone addicted to heroin

Nut — a slang term for a crazy person, or someone overly enthusiastic about something

Habits — customs; the usual way of doing something

Questions:

1. Why do you think Elsa was surprised that her professor invited the class to a party at his house? Would you be surprised if this happened to you?
2. What do you think Elsa should wear to the barbecue? Explain.
3. What are two reasons that might explain why Rick chose to bring potato chips to the party?
4. Do you think that Rick and Jeanette like the same kind of food for dinner? Explain.
5. Have you ever been to a potluck party? What do you think about the custom?

≡ With a Partner

1. Share your ideas about the questions.
2. Together, decide on answers that you both agree on and write them down.
3. Meet with another pair and read your answers to each other.
4. Take turns asking each other to use the vocabulary from the glossary above in a sentence.

THINK ABOUT THIS

1. Do you like to cook?
2. Think of a few reasons why or why not.

☰ Take Sides

1. Go to one side of the room if you like to cook (the other side if you don't like to cook).
2. With everyone on your side of the room, put together a list of reasons why people on your side do (or don't) like to cook.
3. Make sure that you have at least five reasons. Practice by saying five to someone on the same side.
4. Go to the other side of the room and find someone to ask: "What are five reasons why you don't like (or do like) to cook?"
5. Be prepared if your teacher calls on you to give five reasons why people on the other side of the room feel the way they do.
6. In class, talk about whether people on each side of the classroom were of similar genders, nationalities, or ages and why that might be.

····················
BACKGROUND READING

Jeanette's tabbouleh salad and Rick's potato chips are examples of two kinds of popular food in the United States today. International, or ethnic, foods, like Jeanette's Lebanese salad, yogurt (also Middle Eastern), sushi (Japanese), bagels (Jewish), and tacos (Mexican) have become popular with many Americans. Of course, Americans cook many of these dishes their own way. The French might have something to say about the croissants served at McDonald's, for example. Throughout United States history, many "foreign" foods have become all-American favorites. For example, pizza comes from Italy, as everyone knows. Fried chicken, another all-American favorite, was probably first cooked in America by African slaves, who learned deep frying in Africa from Portuguese traders.

Jeanette's grandmother's dish, tabbouleh, is not as popular or well-known as pizza. But it is becoming more popular, especially among Americans who like health food, for it is made from natural, not processed, foods. More and more Americans are interested in fresh foods that have spent more time at the farm than at the factory. Their doctors tell them that they will live longer if they eat less fat, sugar, salt, and red meat. In response, the food industry has developed some new products with labels such as "Lite" and "Low Salt." However, these labels do not always mean that the product is healthy.

What do Americans eat today? Many, such as Rick, prefer junk food: chips, candy, and other packaged foods without much nutritional value. Others prefer "plain old American food," which usually means something like a simply cooked meat with potatoes and vegetables cooked separately. Other Americans, such as Jeanette, have become very interested in foods from around the world and in health foods.

GLOSSARY FOR CASE STUDY AND BACKGROUND READING

Ethnic foods — foods available in the United States that Americans think of as coming from another culture, such as soy sauce

Bagels — round, hard, bread-shaped dough, like donuts

Tacos — thin, crispy, fried, corn dough, usually filled with meat, beans, cheese, sauce, and toppings

Deep frying — frying foods in several inches of oil

Processed foods — foods prepared in factories, such as frozen dinners

Labels — what is written on a package of food

Lite — a food that has had some salt, sugar, alcohol, or fat taken out, according to its manufacturer

Nutritional value — how much energy a food will provide for the body

☰ Quiz Your Partner

1. Make up four generalizations from the Background Reading, some true and some false.

   Example: According to the reading, most Americans prefer "plain old American food." (false)

2. Read your generalizations to your partner and ask him or her to answer "true" or "false." Then give the correct answer.

3. Answer true or false while your partner quizzes you about four generalizations.
4. Quiz each other about the definitions of the vocabulary in the glossary.

   Example: What does *label* mean? (what is written on a package of food)

....
THINK ABOUT THIS

Though milk is the most important food for the health of young children, many adults have stomach problems when they drink cow's milk or eat milk products like cheese. This condition is called *lactose intolerance,* and is especially common among many Asians, East Africans, African Americans, Jews, and Native Americans. Perhaps because lactose intolerance is not very common among Americans of Northern European backgrounds, in the United States milk products are added to many processed foods, such as margarine and bread.

1. Do you have lactose intolerance? What symptoms do you have?
2. Are you allergic to any kind of food?
3. Have you suffered any health problems in the United States that may be related to your change in diet?

≡ With a Partner

1. Share your answers to the questions above.
2. Talk about what you think has caused any changes in your health since coming to the United States.

Interviews and Analysis

 ## Interview Tip: Making Up Good Interview Questions

In this chapter, you will work in a team to find out more about American eating habits. Your team will work on making up half of the questions on the questionnaire, which you will use to interview an American informant. When thinking of good questions, it is important to:

1. **Be specific.**

   Example: "What foods would you avoid if you had a cold?"
   Instead of "What foods are bad?"

2. **Avoid questions with yes/no answers.**

   Example: "How often do you go out to restaurants?"
   Instead of "Do you ever go to restaurants?"

3. **Find out reasons and explanations.**

   Example: "Why are some Americans vegetarians?"
   Instead of "Are some Americans vegetarians?"

4. **Be clear.**

   Example: "Could you tell me about any special religious customs that you observe at mealtime, such as saying prayers before meals or avoiding certain foods?"
   Instead of "Do you observe any special customs when you eat?"

≡ Practice

Based on the four suggestions above, work with a partner to rewrite the following poor questions so that they are better:

1. Could you tell me about American food?
2. Is American food good?
3. Do all Americans eat junk food?
4. Do you like Burger King?

INSTRUCTIONS FOR INTERVIEWS, DISCUSSION, AND PRESENTATIONS

In each corner of the classroom, a sign will be posted with *one* of the following topics: "American Mealtimes," "Food and Health," "Best Restaurants," and "Americans Like...." Go stand in front of the topic that sounds most interesting to you. (Note: if more than six people are interested in the same topic, divide into two (or more) groups no larger than six. Your team will have the job of finding out about the topic from American informants and making some kind of presentation to the class. Your team will follow these six steps, described in more detail below:

- Getting organized
- Writing the questionnaire
- Trying out the questionnaire
- Interviewing American informants
- Team analysis
- Team presentations and quizzes

≡ STEP 1: Getting Organized

Your team will work better if members get to know each other. Do a team interview during which each member stands up, one at a time, and tells teammates three favorite foods. Based on this information, make up a team name.

Next, divide up the roles. Depending on the size of the group, choose among the following roles:

- **Timekeeper** — makes sure that the team finishes its task every day
- **Checker** — makes sure that everyone participates and agrees
- **Secretary** — writes down the interview questions
- **Praiser** — encourages the team and tells members when they do a good job
- **Organizer** — makes sure that everyone on the team has an American informant to interview

☰ STEP 2: Writing the Questionnaire

Find the questionnaire on the following pages that asks about your team's topic and read it over. You will notice that it is not complete.

In your team:

 a. Brainstorm what else you would like to find out about, related to your topic.

 b. Find a partner on your team who likes the same kind of food that you do.

 c. With your partner, choose two of the ideas on the brainstorming list. Work together to write several questions that would help you find out more about these ideas. Other pairs on the team will work on making up questions about the other ideas on the brainstorming list.

 d. When you have finished a draft of your questions, meet with your team to go over everyone's questions, paying careful attention to how clear they are.

 e. As a team, decide on 12 questions to include in the team questionnaire. Choose questions from among those made up by team members *and* from the questionnaire in the book on your team's topic. Show this draft of your questionnaire to you teacher for possible corrections on grammar or wording.

 f. Copy the 12 questions. Make sure everyone on the team has the same questionnaire.

Questionnaire 1: Out-of-class

AMERICAN MEALTIMES

 1. Tell me about breakfast in your home.

 _____

 _____

 2. Tell me what you do for lunch on the weekends.

 _____

 _____

 3. Tell me about dinner in your household.

 _____

 _____

4. When you were growing up, what meals did your family eat together?

_____

5. Did everyone sit in certain chairs? Explain. Where would a guest sit?

_____

_____

6.
7.
8.
9.
10.
11.
12.

Signature of American informant interviewed: _____

Name: _____ Sex: _____

Place of birth: _____ Age: _____

Race, religion, or ethnic background: _____

New vocabulary: _____

Questionnaire 2: Out-of-class

FOOD AND HEALTH

1. What foods, drinks, vitamins, or home remedies are said to be good for:
   a. a cold

   _____

   _____

b. a sore throat

_____

c. an upset stomach

_____

d. a fever

_____

e. a healthy pregnancy

_____

2. Do you think that most Americans would agree with the statement "You can never be too thin"? Explain.

_____

_____

3. What foods and drinks do Americans believe should not be given to babies and very young children?

_____

4. What are health foods? Could you give some examples? Do you eat any health foods?

_____

_____

5.
6.
7.
8.
9.
10.
11.

New vocabulary: _____

Signature of American informant interviewed: _____

Name: _____ Sex: _____

Place of birth: _____ Age: _____

Race, religion, or ethnic background: _____

····················
THINK ABOUT THIS

We think of spaghetti with tomato sauce as a traditional dish from Italy, but noodles were probably invented in China, and the tomato came from the New World. Though not all foods are as cross-cultural as this example, many are.

1. What popular foods in your culture are "borrowed" from another country?

≡ **In a Group with Other Students from Your Cultural Background**

1. Make a list of popular dishes in your native country that have been "borrowed" from other cultures, the way Americans have borrowed pizza from Italy.
2. Write the names of the dishes on the board and present to the class.

Questionnaire 3: Out-of-class

BEST RESTAURANTS

1. We are trying to find out the best places to eat in town. Could you recommend your favorite place to go out for a quick lunch and tell me why you like it?

   _____

   _____

2. What is the best thing to order there?

   _____

3. How are their prices?

   _____

4. What do you think is the best place for pizza?

   _____

5. What else would you order there?

   _____

6.
7.
8.
9.
10.
11.

Signature of American informant interviewed: _____

Name: _____ Sex: _____

Place of birth: _____ Age: _____

Race, religion, or ethnic background: _____

New Vocabulary: _____

....
THINK ABOUT THIS

In the United States, the Thanksgiving holiday in November is associated with eating turkey, a bird native to the Americas.

1. What special foods are associated with certain holidays in your native culture?
2. What special foods are associated with other American holidays? Make notes.

≡ **Have a Contest**

1. Count off with your classmates from one to four. If you are a "one," find the other 1's in the class to form a team. Your classmates will form three other teams. Bring your notes with you.
2. Name your team by finding out one food that everyone on the team hates. Choose the fastest writer on the team to be the secretary.
3. You will have only five minutes. When the teacher gives the signal to begin, start brainstorming a team list of special holiday foods from around the world. Foods associated with American holidays count triple. Use your notes. For each item on the list, include the food (it can be in another language) and the holiday. Spelling does not count.
4. After five minutes, your teacher will tell you to stop. The winning team is the one with the longest list of hoiday foods. They will read their list to the class to make sure that every item is valid.

Questionnaire 4: Out-of-class

AMERICANS LIKE...

To prepare this questionnaire, begin by looking at the list of generalizations that the class made about American eating habits at the beginning of the chapter. Make up a list of questions to find out if these generalizations are true, especially the ones that are marked with a question mark.

Example: Generalization: Americans like to snack.
   Question: Tell me about how often you snack, and what you eat for your snacks.
   Generalization: Americans like Chinese food.
   Questions: Do you like Chinese food? What kinds? Do you think most Americans do?

If your class did not make up generalizations about eating, put together a list of questions to find out what Americans like to eat. The following are some examples:

1. What is your favorite breakfast?

2. What are some of the traditional foods in your family that are prepared for the different holidays?
3. When you were a child, what foods did your mother prepare as a special treat?
4. Do you know if this part of the country is famous for any dishes in particular? What would you recommend?

Signature of American informant interviewed: _____

Name: _____ Sex: _____

Place of birth: _____ Age: _____

Race, religion, or ethnic background: _____

New vocabulary: _____

≡ STEP 3: Trying Out the Questionnaire.

Divide into pairs and use the team's questionnaire to interview each other. Because the questionnaire was written for American informants, you may have to change the wording of some of the questions to ask your classmates. Then share the most interesting things that you learned from your partner with the rest of the team. The secretary should take notes, since this information may be used later.

Talk over with the team how well the questions worked. Decide whether to change any. Discuss plans to interview American informants. Instead of interviewing an American informant by yourself, you can work with the partner you interviewed and together interview two Americans.

≡ STEP 4: Interviewing American Informants.

Interview an American informant, using the team's questionnaire. If you work with your partner, one person can take notes while the other asks the questions in the first interview. Then switch roles for the other interview.

☰ STEP 5: Team Analysis.

After your interview(s), meet with your team to talk over how well the questionnaire worked. Share and discuss the information that was learned from the interviews. One way to do this is to have everyone in the group give a summary of the most interesting points. If the team is large, work in pairs to share this information and prepare a summary for the team.

Working as a whole team, come up with a list of the main ideas that were learned from the interviews. Compare this information to what teammates learned when they interviewed each other.

☰ STEP 6: Team Presentations and Quizzes.

Your team will decide how to present what you learned about your topic to the whole class. Your team's presentation should also include one or more of the following:

- A chart
- A graph
- A handout
- A skit
- A photographic exhibit or album
- A team-made video
- A cooking demonstration
- Food samples

Following your team presentation, hand out a quiz about your topic to your classmates to find out how well your team communicated their information. Make up five to ten generalizations about your team presentation and ask your classmates to rate them "true" or "false." Correct them in class.

JOURNAL

Write about your experience working in a team to complete the activities for this chapter. In what ways did you find the team helpful? What could your team have done to work better together? How did you function as a team member? What could you have done to help the team function better? How did your work in a team change the way you thought about American eating customs?

....

THINK ABOUT THIS

Every state in the United States has a law about how old customers must be to buy liquor.

1. Do you know what age you must be to buy liquor in the state in which you are living?
2. What is the reason for these laws?
3. Write down three customs or laws about buying or drinking alcohol where you come from.

☰ With a Partner from Another Cultural Background

1. Share the three customs that you wrote down. Talk about their advantages and disadvantages.
2. After listening to your partner share his or her customs, repeat these in your own words. This is called paraphrasing.
3. Which customs or laws make the most sense to you? Talk over with your partner how you feel about what society should do about alcohol use.

≡ With the Whole Class

Muslims do not drink liquor; according to their religion, it is *taboo*. The Muslim religion also considers pork taboo, as does the Jewish religion. What meats are eaten, and what meats are considered taboo in your native culture? Go around the room answering this question, while a classmate or your teacher fills out this chart on the board:

MEATS EATEN EVERYWHERE	TABOO MEATS EVERYWHERE	MEATS TABOO IN CERTAIN CULTURES	
Meats: (list)	Taboo Meats:	Meat:	Taboo in:

Additional Activities

TABLE MANNERS CHECK-OFF

Suppose that you have invited a friend to your parents' home for a family dinner. During the meal, your friend does the following things. Next to each, check off whether you would rate her behavior "Good Manners," "Bad Manners," or "Neither." Ask an American or a classmate from another country to rate the same behaviors and check off their responses in a different-colored ink, pencil, or marker.

TABLE MANNERS: GOOD, BAD, OR NEITHER?			
	Good	Bad	Neither
1. Your friend remains standing until shown a chair.			
2. She helps herself to some meat from a bowl on the table.			
3. As soon as she has food on her plate, she begins eating.			
4. She talks with food in her mouth.			

	Good	Bad	Neither
5. She puts her napkin on her lap.			
6. She mops the gravy up with her roll.			
7. She makes slurping sounds while eating.			
8. She keeps a hand in her lap while eating.			
9. She drinks her soup from the bowl without a spoon.			
10. She picks up a roll with her left hand.			
11. She comments on how good the food is.			
12. She asks for the recipe.			
13. She finishes everything on her plate.			
14. She asks for a second helping.			
15. She puts her elbows on the table.			
16. She tells about a bloody accident on the TV news.			
17. She licks some gravy off her fingers.			
18. She picks up a chicken wing with her hands.			
19. She quietly leaves the table to use the bathroom.			
20. She eats quickly.			
21. When offered seconds, she says "No thanks."			
22. She belches after the meal.			
23. She helps clear the table.			
24. She says "Thank you" to your parents.			
25. She leaves right after dinner.			

RESTAURANT REVIEW

With the members of your team, have a meal at a local restaurant so that you can write a restaurant review. Prepare by reading a restaurant review column which usually appears weekly in the local newspaper. Take notes on the food, service, and decor. Afterward, talk it over and compare notes. Write a review or reviews, modeled after those published by the newspaper's restaurant critic.

Photography Credits

All photos by Carol Palmer and Andrew Brilliant with the exception of the following:

Dave Swierkosz: pp. 15, 56, 85, 94, 123, 165, 204, 206, 212

Christine Heckly: p. 81

David Frasier: p. 165

Rhoda Sidney/Stock Boston: p. 101

Comstock, Inc.: p. 107, 197

FPG International: p. 140

Eric Liebowitz: p. 180

Jeff Greenburg: p. 184

AP/Wide World Photos: p. 14 (top), 200

Peter Menzel/Stock Boston: p. 218

Jerry Howard/Stock Boston: p. 214

Steven Rosenthal/The Boston Children's Museum: p. 14 (middle)